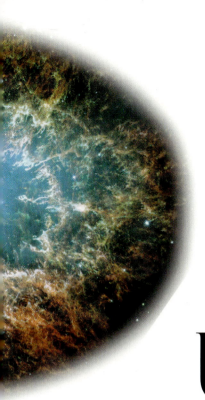

GUIDE TO THE

UNIVERSE

INSTITUTE FOR
CREATION RESEARCH

Dallas, Texas
www.ICR.org

GUIDE TO THE UNIVERSE

First printing: November 2016

All Scripture quotations are from the New King James Version.

ISBN: 978-1-935587-82-8
Library of Congress Catalog Number: 2016945712

Please visit our website for other books and resources: www.ICR.org

Printed in the United States of America.

Contents

ORIGINS OF AN ORCHESTRATED UNIVERSE 8

WHAT DOES THE BIBLE SAY ABOUT SPACE? 10

ASTRONOMERS IN HISTORY 12

THE COPERNICAN REVOLUTION 14

ISAAC NEWTON, FATHER OF PHYSICS 16

THE ACHIEVEMENTS OF ALBERT EINSTEIN 18

HOW BIG IS OUR UNIVERSE? 20

ORIGINS OF THE BIG BANG 22

CREATION COSMOLOGIES 24

OUR PERFECTLY BALANCED SOLAR SYSTEM 26

THE SUN: SUPPORTING LIFE ON EARTH 28

MELTING ON MERCURY 30

VENUS, EARTH'S SISTER PLANET 32

OUR EXTRAORDINARY EARTH 36

THE MAKING OF THE MOON 38

MYSTERIOUS MARS 40

JUPITER, A GIANT JEWEL 42

Celebrating Saturn 44

Unexpected Uranus 46

Neptune, Blue as the Sea 48

Pluto, the Dwarf Planet 50

Magnetic Fields and Why They Matter 52

Studying the Stars 54

Blue Stars and Star Formation 56

Stargazing Basics for Beginners 60

Starlight and Time 62

Outer Space and Other Marvels 64

Asteroids, Comets, and Other Celestial Mysteries 66

Shedding Light on Black Holes 68

Gazing at Galaxies 70

Naturalistic Speculations 72

Evidence for a Young Universe 74

NASA's Intriguing History 78

A Tribute to the Hubble Space Telescope 80

Exploring Space Probes 82

The Space Shuttle Program 84

Fascinating Space Facts 86

Man on the Moon 88

How to Be an Astronaut 90

The Human Body in Space 92

Sending Out Satellites 94

Science Fiction vs. Reality 96

Building the International Space Station 98

Life on the International Space Station 100

Photos from Space 102

Caution: Astronauts at Work 104

Searching for Life 106

God's Attributes Are Clearly Seen 108

Index 110

Contributors 112

Acknowledgment 113

Publication Credits and Endnotes 114

Image Credits 115

About ICR 117

Origins of an Orchestrated Universe

When you woke up this morning, did you gasp to see the sun shining once again? Probably not. We see the sun doing its job faithfully each day. As the world turns, this bright golden star appears to move across the sky from east to west—marking time even better than a clock. And it's not the only heavenly body with a trust-worthy track record. The movements of majestic planets and our moon can be predicted years ahead of time with great precision. All exist in just the right positions at just the right times and in stunningly beautiful ways for our distinct benefit.

TWO WORLDVIEWS

Many claim these wonders of the universe resulted from a cosmic accident, an apparently causeless beginning. Naturalistic scientists believe that natural processes formed the universe over 13 billion years ago. They think such a long period of time allowed order to come from disorder.

Meanwhile, the Bible's genealogies and historical timeline indicate that God supernaturally created the universe about 6,000 years ago. Scriptures tell us that the intricate workings of the universe reflect God's masterful design, and He created it all with great purpose.

With two dramatically different worldviews, how can we know who has the right answer?

"Everyday experiences, such as breaking watches and spilling milk, remind us that order does not happen by itself. In fact, our entire universe demonstrates that same truth. The earth's rotation, the moon cycle, and the changing seasons are just a few of the ordered processes observable in nature. These processes don't happen randomly—God causes them."[1]

—Dr. Henry M. Morris III
CEO, Institute for Creation Research

EVIDENCE FOR CREATION

Many aspects of the universe confirm the biblical timescale and point to the need for an all-powerful Creator to perform such incredible works. This book shows how naturalistic ideas violate laws of physics and ignore contrary evidence.

Our Creator didn't leave us alone staring up at the sky to wonder about His existence. He wants us to know the truth about ourselves and our origins, so He provided His very own eyewitness account in the Bible. He inspired human authors to take down the notes in words we can understand (2 Samuel 23:2; 2 Peter 1:21; 2 Timothy 3:16).

THE CREATION ACCOUNT

The opening chapters of Genesis tell us that an intentional, powerful, loving, and holy God created the universe and everything in it. He is the great First Cause who needed no cause because He is infinite—the only Person with no beginning. He exists outside of time (Psalm 90:2).

"In the beginning God created the heavens and the earth" (Genesis 1:1).

God created everything in the universe in only six days, and He made the planets, stars, moons, and other celestial bodies on Day 4.

"Then God said, 'Let there be lights in the firmament of the heavens to divide the day from the night; and let them be for signs and seasons, and for days and years; and let them be for lights in the firmament of the heavens to give light on the earth'; and it was so. Then God made two great lights: the greater light to rule the day, and the lesser light to rule the night. He made the stars also" (Genesis 1:14-16).

"For by Him all things were created that are in heaven and that are on earth, visible and invisible, whether thrones or dominions or principalities or powers. All things were created through Him and for Him." (Colossians 1:16)

DAY 1

DAY 2

DAY 3

DAY 4

DAY 5

DAY 6

THE HEAVENS DECLARE

The Bible says that the heavens declare God's glory (Psalm 19:1), and we can hear their proclamation from every part of the world. Every sky full of stars, every planet that makes us marvel, and every day that greets us with a kiss from the sun shouts of God! The question is, are we listening?

What Does the Bible Say about Space?

While the Bible doesn't provide comprehensive information on space, it does give us insights on the universe and God's role in its creation. We can trust that God's Word is always true and reliable—in matters of science as well as theology.

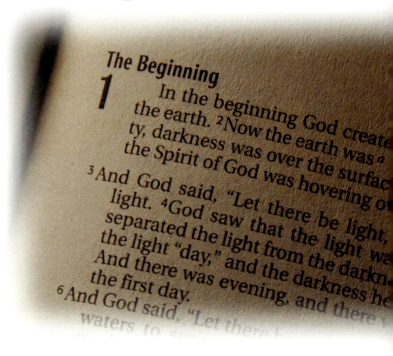

The Beginning
1 In the beginning God create the earth. ²Now the earth was a ty, darkness was over the surfac the Spirit of God was hovering o ³And God said, "Let there be light, light. ⁴God saw that the light we separated the light from the darkn the light "day," and the darkness he And there was evening, and there the first day. ⁶And God said, "Let there waters to se

THE HEAVENS

"In the beginning God created the heavens and the earth" (Genesis 1:1). Even a young child understands this. God crafted what we see when we look up as well as the ground we stand on. We see an atmosphere with birds and clouds, and on clear nights planets, stars, galaxies—and sometimes even comets or meteorites. God deserves credit for all this. "Praise Him, sun and moon; praise Him, all you stars of light!" (Psalm 148:3).

WHAT IS THE FIRMAMENT?

Genesis 1:6 says that God made a "firmament." What does this mean? Genesis reveals that "God called the firmament Heaven" (Genesis 1:8). Then on Day 4, God made stars, saying, "Let there be lights in the firmament of the heavens" (Genesis 1:14). So, the firmament includes space for all the stellar lights—everything from brown dwarfs to blue supergiants. And in Genesis 1:20, we learn that the firmament also includes space for flying creatures. Even in Psalm 19:1, the words "firmament" and "heavens" refer to the same thing.

THE STUFF OF SPACE

The word translated "firmament" comes from a Hebrew word that refers to an expanse of emptiness and/or stretched-out thinness. If space consisted of nothing, then how could light waves travel through it? Some suggest that space is comprised of an extremely thin substance not made of atoms called *ether*. While we wait for more research on the stuff of space, we know that God made it with just the right properties to house stars and transmit light.

God's Purpose for Sky Lights

Genesis 1:14-18 tells us why God created the sun, moon, and stars. First, they light the earth. The sun "rules" the day. Its light powers plant growth that feeds creatures great and small, and it inspires us to remember our great Provider. The moon "rules" the night and with the stars graces us with an evening glow in the midst of the darkness. Also, these sky lights set daily rhythms for countless plants and animals and help us keep count of our lives and of history. Since creation, people have used the rising and setting of the sun, the phases of the moon, and positioning of the stars to track time—they're the basis for our days, months, and years. God also created the sun, moon, and stars to divide light from darkness.

"The heavens declare the glory of God; and the firmament shows His handiwork. Day unto day utters speech, and night unto night reveals knowledge. There is no speech nor language where their voice is not heard." (Psalm 19:1-3)

Signs in the Sky

According to Genesis 1:14, God intended the sun, moon, and stars to serve as signs. Signs of what? Do zodiacal motions, eclipses, and apparent mergers of various stellar bodies offer hidden meanings? The word "sign" refers to a distinguishing mark or miraculous proof. So, God made heavenly bodies not to hide secrets but to plainly reveal something…or Someone. Our great Creator must be even brighter and more immense than His mere handiwork because "by His Spirit He adorned the heavens" (Job 26:13).

Spreading Out the Heavens

Job 9:8 says, "He alone spreads out the heavens." This is the first of several references in the Bible to God "spreading" or "stretching" out the heavens. Some suggest this refers to an expanding universe that fits Big Bang models. But all of the passages make it clear this was the direct result of the Word of God, not the result of a primeval explosion. And a few astrophysicists find reasons to doubt that the universe is still expanding. We cannot claim these verses prove God is currently expanding the universe; better data may indicate that the universe maintains a constant size. These passages may suggest an expanding universe or, more likely, simply the vast extension of space.

Astronomers in History

We can scientifically study the universe because God created it in an orderly way. If the universe were the result of random processes, it would be impossible to draw dependable conclusions because nothing would be consistent. Thankfully, God formed celestial bodies that function in predictable ways within the principles of mathematics and physics. He also gave humans brains that can reason and apply these principles to discover the wonders of His creation. Some of the most famous observers of the universe used these God-given gifts to further their knowledge and understanding of the heavens, and we continue to build on their discoveries. Let's meet some of these astronomers.

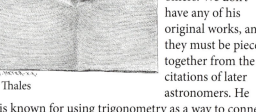

Thales

THALES (C. 624–C. 546 B.C.)

Thales was one of the first Greek astronomers. We don't have any of his original works, and so they must be pieced together from the citations of later astronomers. He is known for using trigonometry as a way to connect astronomy and mathematics. He may have successfully predicted a solar eclipse in 585 B.C. He also measured the apparent diameter of the sun and recognized the importance of the Ursa Minor constellation—which holds the North Star—for seafarers. As was common in that day, Thales believed the earth was flat.

Pythagoras

PYTHAGORAS (C. 570–C. 495 B.C.)

Greek philosopher and mathematician Pythagoras supposedly first proposed that the earth is a sphere based on the observation that the other heavenly bodies are spherical. He suggested that the movement of the planetary bodies could be described mathematically, a precursor to modern astronomical physics.

PLATO (C. 428–C. 348 B.C.)

Plato, a Greek philosopher, taught that the stars, sun, moon, and other celestial bodies were round and fixed on transparent spheres that surrounded Earth, a theory known as *geocentrism*. Supposedly, these spheres rotated within each other, causing the movements of the heavens.

ARISTOTLE (384–322 B.C.)

Aristotle studied under Plato. Like Plato, he believed in geocentrism and that the planets and stars were perfect spheres, though the earth was not. He thought that since a circle is a perfect shape, the celestial bodies must move in circles.

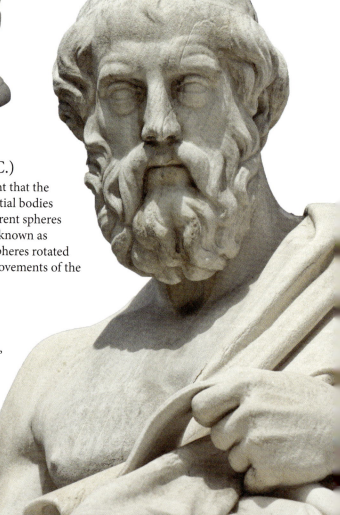

Aristotle   Plato

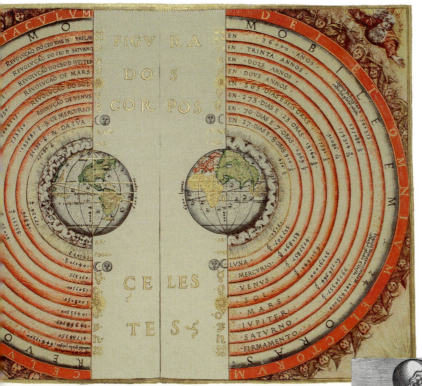

Ptolemaic geocentric conception, from a 1568 manuscript

ERATOSTHENES (276–194 B.C.)

Eratosthenes calculated the size of the earth with significant accuracy. By observing the difference in the angle of shadows in different towns at the same time of the day, he noted that the sun's rays fell nearly vertically at noon in the town of Syene, Egypt, but fell about 7.2 degrees at noon in Alexandria. Applying these observations, Eratosthenes arrived at measurements of the earth's circumference that come surprisingly close to the numbers we have from satellite technology today.

Eratosthenes

PTOLEMY (C. 100–C. 170 B.C.)

Ptolemy developed a model of the universe that was used for over 1,000 years, all the way through the 16th and 17th centuries. Plato's idea that celestial bodies move in small circles did not match the math, so Greek astronomers Hipparchus and Apollonius developed the theory of epicycles—the idea that the sun, moon, and other celestial bodies move in small circles within their orbits. But even epicycles did not explain all their movements. To compensate for the theory's weakness, Ptolemy began developing epicycles within epicycles, resulting in a very complex model of celestial motion.

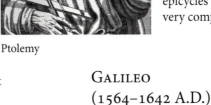

Ptolemy

HERACLIDES (387–312 B.C.)

The philosopher Heraclides proposed that the apparent daily revolution of the stars could be due to Earth rotating on an axis. This contradicted Aristotle's model of the cosmos.

COPERNICUS (1473–1543 A.D.)

Nicolaus Copernicus challenged millennia-old ideas about the cosmos with his publication of *On the Revolutions of the Celestial Spheres*. He presented mathematical evidence that placed the sun at the center of the solar system, not the earth—a concept known as *heliocentrism*. This confronted the geocentrism of his day. His work was so controversial and different from mainstream thought that it took several centuries for popular culture to accept it. This shift in viewpoint is called the *Copernican Revolution*.

GALILEO (1564–1642 A.D.)

About 100 years after Copernicus, the Western world was still in an uproar over the astronomer's conclusions. Then came Galileo, who is known for developing a powerful telescope that he used to confirm and promote Copernicus' theory. Church authorities forced him to recant his loyalty to Copernican ideas and then put him under house arrest for the rest of his life. However, Copernicus' and Galileo's works were already out in the public, and eventually the Western world accepted heliocentrism.

Galileo

Copernicus

The Copernican Revolution

Nicolaus Copernicus sparked the Copernican Revolution, one of the biggest shifts of scientific thought in history. He revived and popularized the idea that the planets revolve around the sun, not the earth. This began the transition from geocentrism (an Earth-centered universe) to heliocentrism (a sun-centered solar system) and ushered in a new view of cosmology.

GREEK PHILOSOPHY

Early Greek philosophy held to geocentrism, the idea that the earth resides at the center of the universe and all the visible planets as well as the sun orbit around it. Plato and Aristotle largely developed this model. They assumed that the planets travel in perfect circles because they thought a circle was the perfect shape. Though Aristarchus of Samos proposed a sun-centered solar system in the 3rd century B.C., the idea did not catch on.

Later, Greek philosopher Ptolemy realized that this did not fit with his observations of the heavens and developed the theory of epicycles. This theory proposed that the planets make little orbital circles within their larger orbital paths. It remained a popular belief for centuries—until Nicolaus Copernicus entered the scene.

> **OVERVIEW**
>
> Copernicus publishes *On the Revolutions of the Celestial Spheres*—1543
>
> Galileo confirms Copernicus' theory with his telescope—1609
>
> Galileo publishes *Dialogue*—1632
>
> Galileo is condemned as a heretic—1633

Ptolemaic system (above)

Comparison of geocentrism and heliocentrism (left)

Statue of Nicolaus Copernicus (right)

Earth
Moon
Mercury
Venus
Sun
Mars
Jupiter
Saturn

COPERNICUS

Nicolaus Copernicus was born in Poland to a merchant in 1473. He was only 10 years old when his father died, so his uncle adopted him. At 18, he enrolled at the University of Krakow, where he became interested in astronomy. During his later education at the University of Bologna, he lived with an astronomy professor who challenged Ptolemy's model and sowed the seeds of his pivotal work *On the Revolutions of the Celestial Spheres* in Copernicus' mind.

> "I am aware that a philosopher's ideas are not subject to the judgment of ordinary persons, because it is his endeavor to seek the truth in all things, to the extent permitted to human reason by God."
>
> — Nicolaus Copernicus

Sometime before 1514, he penned an important essay called *Commentariolus,* which became the first formal articulation of his heliocentric theory. In 1539, a young mathematician from the University of Wittenberg came to study with Copernicus and encouraged him to publish his theories. The young mathematician helped with publication, and Copernicus held the first edition of his book on the day of his death, May 24, 1543.

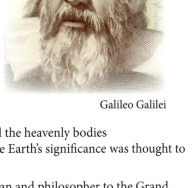

GALILEO

Galileo Galilei was born in Italy in 1564 not long after the death of Copernicus. He studied at a monastery during his childhood and then attended the University of Pisa to study medicine. However, he never finished his medical degree. He moved his studies over to mathematics, and his skills flourished so greatly that he became a teacher of geometry, mechanics, and astronomy at the University of Padua when he was 28.

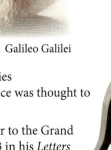

Galileo Galilei

At 45, he constructed a telescope and used it to discover Jupiter's four moons. This had a profound effect upon cosmology because it contradicted the idea that all the heavenly bodies revolve around Earth. This new view was resisted because Earth's significance was thought to be diminished if geocentrism wasn't true.

Eventually Galileo assumed the position of mathematician and philosopher to the Grand Duke of Tuscany and publicly expressed his support of Copernicus in 1613 in his *Letters on the Sunspots.* However, the church did not take kindly to Galileo's theories and, after banning Copernicus' book in 1616, ordered Galileo not to teach or defend heliocentrism. But Galileo simply kept quiet for a while, then published his highly controversial *Dialogue Concerning the Two Great World Systems* in 1632. The publication had life-changing consequences for the scientist. The next year the church banned his book, convicted him of heresy, and forced him to recant. In 1634, he was sent to house arrest in Arcetri just outside France. He died there in 1642.

> "I do not feel obliged to believe that the same God who has endowed us with sense, reason, and intellect has intended us to forgo their use."
>
> — Galileo Galilei

Cristiano Banti's 1857 painting *Galileo Facing the Roman Inquisition*

Isaac Newton, Father of Physics

Many consider Isaac Newton (1643-1727) to be the father of physics, the one who brought all the motions of the universe together into the three universal laws of motion. He also conducted groundbreaking research into the nature of color and light, and notable studies in theology and philosophy. Even during his lifetime, fellow scientists sometimes referred to Newton as the greatest genius who ever lived. While this may be debatable, his research still stands as a landmark of scientific thought.

Sir Isaac Newton

CHILDHOOD AND EDUCATION

Newton was born in Woolsthorpe, a small English country town, in 1643. His mother was recently widowed. He graduated from King's School for boys, where he developed a love for chemistry, and then moved on to Cambridge. He learned the standard curriculum there but spent all of his spare time studying cutting-edge theories in science and philosophy. After graduation, Newton retreated to private study. When the plague subsided, he resumed his Cambridge education and received a Master of Arts. A research paper he shared with a friend landed him a Cambridge professorship at the age of 27.

OPTICKS

As a Cambridge professor, Newton taught courses on optics. During that time, he designed and constructed a reflecting telescope to delve further into his study of optics—his first significant scientific achievement. Newton's telescope so impressed the Royal Society that they asked him for a demonstration. Newton published *Opticks* in 1704. It remains a milestone in scientific thought.

Robert Hooke, who coined the biological use of the term "cell," objected to Newton's conclusions, beginning a fierce lifelong rivalry between the two scientists. Years later, Newton allegedly used one of Hooke's ideas regarding planetary motion as a springboard for developing his own groundbreaking studies in the laws of motion.

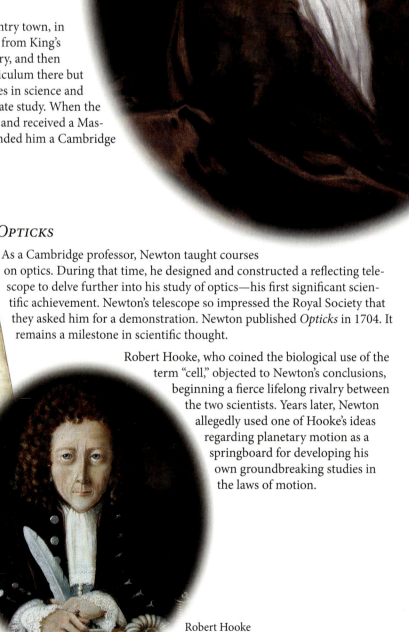

Robert Hooke

THE *PRINCIPIA*

Newton and Hooke exchanged letters in which Hooke suggested that planetary orbits might be explained using an inverse square formula. Newton explored this possibility and by 1680 developed his conclusions on planetary motion. In 1684, a scientist of the Royal Society visited him and casually asked what a planet's orbit would look like if Hooke's suspicions were correct. Newton confidently said, "An ellipse." The scientist, impressed by his response, offered to pay for Newton to publish his work on the matter. So, in 1687 Newton published *Philosophiæ Naturalis Principia Mathematica* (*The Mathematical Principles of Natural Philosophy*), one of the most influential science books in history, and it pushed him onto the international stage.

NEWTON'S LAWS OF MOTION

1. Objects at rest will remain at rest and objects in motion will remain in motion unless acted upon by an outside force.
2. **F** = m**a** (Force = mass x acceleration).
3. For every action, there is an equal and opposite reaction.

DID YOU KNOW?

F = m**a** is Newton's groundbreaking equation that states the net force on an object is equal to its mass times acceleration. Newton used it to calculate lunar tides, the bulging of the earth's equator, planetary ellipses, and many other physical effects.

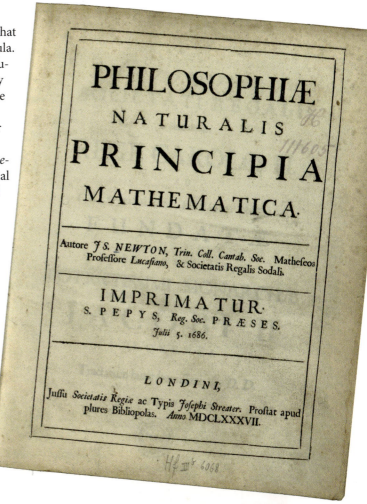

PHILOSOPHIÆ
NATURALIS
PRINCIPIA
MATHEMATICA.

Autore *JS. NEWTON*, *Trin. Coll. Cantab. Soc.* Mathefeos
Profeffore Lucafiano, & Societatis Regalis Sodali.

IMPRIMATUR.
S. PEPYS, *Reg. Soc.* PRÆSES.
Julii 5. 1686.

LONDINI,
Juffu *Societatis Regiæ* ac Typis *Jofephi Streater.* Proftat apud
plures Bibliopolas. *Anno* MDCLXXXVII.

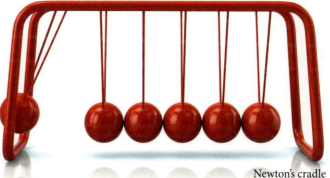

Newton's cradle

ADDITIONAL ACHIEVEMENTS

Newton's breakthroughs earned him international esteem, and he became quite involved in political affairs. He represented Cambridge in Parliament, became warden of the Mint, served as president of the Royal Society, and received a knighthood. In 1727, he died at 84 years old.

"It is the perfection of God's works that they are all done with the greatest simplicity."

—Newton

How Big Is Our Universe?

"Indeed My hand has laid the foundation of the earth, and My right hand has stretched out the heavens; when I call to them, they stand up together." (Isaiah 48:13)

How big is our universe? Perhaps a better question is: How big is the *observable* universe? Astronomers believe the visible universe is a spherical shape more than 550,000,000,000,000,000,000,000 miles in diameter—that's over 500 sextillion miles! And there may be even more universe beyond what we can see.

It's hard to comprehend the incredible distances in outer space. How did our universe get that big? It says in Genesis and Isaiah that God created the stars on Day 4 of the creation week…and He stretched out the heavens. God actually stretched out space!

MEASURING SPACE: THE AU, THE LIGHT-YEAR, AND THE PARSEC

One of the units astronomers use to measure space is called an *astronomical unit* (AU). An AU is the average distance from Earth to the sun—about 93 million miles. If we could take a rocket ship beyond our solar system, we'd see that our sun and planets are only a tiny part of the Milky Way galaxy. We'd also find that the distances are so great that the AU doesn't work very well—it's just too small. So astronomers use light-years and parsecs to measure those distances. One light-year is about 5,880,000,000,000 miles (5.88 trillion miles), and a *parsec* is about 19 trillion miles (3.26 light-years). Astronomers use parsecs to measure the distances between stars, and kiloparsecs (1,000 parsecs) and megaparsecs (1,000,000 parsecs) for the incredibly vast distances between galaxies.

DID YOU KNOW?

A light-year is a *distance* measurement not a *time* measurement. One light-year is a distance of almost six trillion miles!

New Horizons

HOW DO ASTRONOMERS MEASURE THESE GREAT DISTANCES?

To measure how far away stars are, astronomers use a method of measurement called a *parallax*. To understand it try this: stretch out one of your arms in front of you and hold up your index finger. Close one eye and look at the background behind your finger with your other eye; switch eyes and your finger will visually shift from one side to the other. This movement happens because your eyes are about three inches apart. The distance your finger appears to shift relative to the background is a parallax.

Astronomers carefully measure the position of a nearby star relative to the more distant stars behind it. Six months later, when the earth is at the opposite side of its orbit around the sun (a change in Earth's position of two AUs—about 186 million miles), the astronomers measure the nearby star's position a second time and compare it to the same stars that reside behind it. If the star is rather close to Earth, a clear parallax—the shift in position—will be visible. Using the amount of shift in the star's position and the parallax angle, astronomers can calculate the star's distance from Earth. It's geometry at work!

COSMIC DISTANCES

The moon is	238,000 miles from Earth
The sun is one astronomical unit (AU)	93,000,000 miles (93 million miles) from Earth
Pluto is	3,700,000,000 miles (3.7 billion miles) from Earth
A light-year is	5,880,000,000,000 miles (6 trillion miles) in length
A parsec is	19,000,000,000,000 miles (19 trillion miles) in length
The Alpha Centauri star system is	25,690,000,000,000 miles (25 trillion miles) from Earth
The Milky Way galaxy is	588,000,000,000,000,000 miles (6 quadrillion miles) across
The visible universe is	550,000,000,000,000,000,000,000 miles (500 sextillion miles) across

Origins of the Big Bang

How did the universe begin? Some believe an explosion brought it all into existence—a Big Bang from essentially nothing, with no apparent cause, 13.8 billion years ago.

In the 1920s, astronomer Edwin Hubble observed clues that seemed to suggest the universe is expanding. If you "rewind" that expansion, you could assume that every galaxy moved from a common central starting point to its current position. Secular scientists used this idea to conclude that the universe resulted from an enormous explosion.

Edwin Hubble

The Big Bang model is popular, but it has made almost no successful predictions, which is what a scientific model is supposed to do. In fact, the original Big Bang model had three very serious problems—horizon, flatness, and monopole problems. And despite various attempts to tweak the model to account for the observations that don't fit, the Big Bang still has major challenges.

THE COSMOLOGICAL PRINCIPLE

The Big Bang model rests on a basic assumption called the *cosmological principle.* This principle assumes that matter and energy are spread out uniformly in the universe and that there are no special directions in space. This means that the universe would have no center and no boundary. Without the cosmological principle, there is no Big Bang. However, no observations actually support this principle. Also, a newfound group of quasars— bright and massive quasi-stellar radio sources—are spaced four times farther apart than the cosmological principle predicted. This has caused even secular scientists to question it.

THE HORIZON PROBLEM

Some people object to a recent creation because of the apparent distant starlight problem (see pages 62-63). But the Big Bang has its own time-distance problem called the *horizon problem*. With the Big Bang, the universe supposedly started out very small with large temperature fluctuations from place to place. But the cosmic microwave background (CMB) radiation—a faint microwave radiation coming from all directions in space—seems to have very nearly uniform temperatures, with only minor variations. Secular cosmologists had to argue that radiant energy—moving at the speed of light—traveled from "hot" areas to "cold" areas, evening out the temperature. But the alleged 13.8 billion years since the Big Bang don't allow enough time for this to happen.

THE FLATNESS PROBLEM

The large-scale geometry of the universe is generally thought to be "flat." But in the Big Bang model a flat universe would be highly improbable because this would require an unbelievably precise balance between gravity and the universe's expansion. The slightest imbalance would make it impossible for life to exist. The precise relationship between gravity and expansion seems to indicate fine-tuning and design, but how does that fit if everything started with a giant explosion?

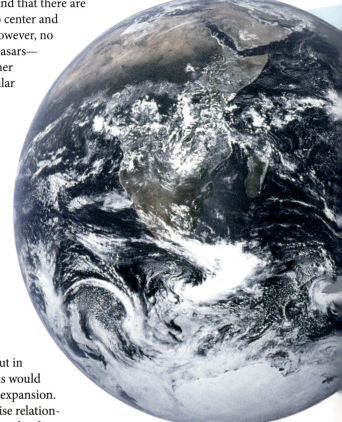

THE MONOPOLE PROBLEM

A magnetic *monopole* is a hypothetical particle that has only one magnetic pole. According to certain theories, these particles should be produced at extremely high temperatures—the kind that would have occurred during the Big Bang. Yet not a single monopole has ever been discovered. Magnetic poles always come in pairs—one north and one south.

NOTHING?

INFLATION

When confronted with the horizon, flatness, and monopole problems, secular scientists retrofitted the Big Bang to accommodate them by adding a concept called *inflation*, a super-accelerated, faster-than-light expansion of space. They say that this could have evened out the temperature differences in the CMB and that space only *seems* flat because it was enormously "blown up" by inflation. This inflation would also supposedly have spread magnetic monopoles so far out in space that they would almost certainly never be observed.

But inflation is really just a speculation and has serious problems of its own. In fact, modern inflation theory has become so strange—with ideas like a "multiverse" with an infinite number of universes—that former proponents of the theory now criticize it.

THE ASYMMETRY PROBLEM

A faint microwave radiation called *cosmic microwave background* (CMB) radiation appears to come from all directions in space. Big Bang defenders believe that an early inflating universe produced the CMB. However, other causes can also explain it. Plus, the Big Bang never predicted a newly discovered detail—the CMB is lopsided. One half of the universe has temperature and density variation patches, and the other half is quite smooth. Nobody yet knows how any type of Big Bang could accomplish that.

THE ANTIMATTER PROBLEM

The universe contains very little antimatter, which is like ordinary matter but with opposite charges. (For example, an antiproton has a negative charge.) The Big Bang model maintains that the early universe was made up only of electromagnetic radiation since it was too hot for matter to exist. As the universe expanded and cooled, radiation, in the form of colliding photons, was transformed into ordinary matter. Making matter from radiation is possible in particle accelerators. However, every time we make matter from radiation, we get a precisely equal amount of antimatter. If the Big Bang were true, we'd expect to find equal amounts of matter and antimatter. But we don't.

Big Bang proponents claim our universe sprang into existence out of essentially nothing—without an apparent cause. According to the Bible, however, in the beginning there was no Big Bang...only the Word of God (John 1:1-3), the Lord Jesus Christ, calling the whole universe into existence!

"In the beginning was the Word, and the Word was with God, and the Word was God. He was in the beginning with God. All things were made through Him, and without Him nothing was made that was made." (John 1:1-3)

Creation Cosmologies

Cosmologists theorize about the basic parts of the universe, how they interact, where they came from, and how they could end. These theories—known as *cosmologies*—involve equations that include known, unknown, and even unknowable variables. The equations are used to find possible answers to questions such as: How fast does light travel? How is matter distributed in the universe? Does the universe have an outer edge and a center, or does it go on forever and have no center?

Cosmologies and Equations

Physicists can adjust the many variables of cosmology equations to fit their observations. So, even if an equation seems to work, that doesn't necessarily mean it's correct. It's simply one possibility among many others.

Secular cosmologies attempt to describe a universe without God, where miracles never happened—even though their own origin theories require miracles. But Bible-respecting physicists have suggested cosmologies that include God, supernatural events, and even a 6,000-year-old universe. One of them involves a mysterious object called a *white hole*.

White Hole Cosmology

A white hole would work like a black hole in reverse. Instead of pulling matter and light inward with intense gravity like a black hole, a white hole blasts matter and energy outward. Once set in motion, a white hole could cause a tremendous amount of matter and energy to appear. A white hole better explains the universe's origin than the Big Bang since it presents fewer problems. In contrast, Big Bang cosmologies introduce all kinds of problems, and we explain some of them on pages 22-23. Even secular scientists agree that white holes are possible based on known physics.

CARMELIAN COSMOLOGY

Secular physicist Moshe Carmeli proposed a cosmology with five dimensions of reality—length, width, height, time, and velocity. Bible-believing physicist John Hartnett applied this model to the whole universe. It describes an extremely fast expansion of space during creation, with clocks moving rapidly at the edge of expanding space.

In this model, light from distant galaxies reached Earth in a short time as measured by our clocks. But this same light takes billions of years to reach us when measured by cosmic clocks—a mind-bending "both/and" space-time possibility. The model is an extension of the known physics of general relativity, but the details of how it may have worked reside in complicated mathematical formulas.

SPEED-OF-LIGHT CONVENTION

Creation cosmologies attempt to describe a universe made by God only several thousand years ago, like the Bible teaches. Astrophysicist Dr. Jason Lisle described one such possibility. He suggested that Einstein's convention for the one-way speed of light was wrong. Page 63 describes how a new convention could solve creation's apparent light-time challenge.

Quasar 3c 273

DR. RUSSELL HUMPHREYS' MODEL

Creation physicist Dr. Russell Humphreys used white holes as a way to describe the Genesis creation. He used Einstein's equations of general relativity, but unlike secular cosmologies, which assume that the universe has no edge or center, his model assumed that the earth is near the center of a bounded universe, as the Bible implies. In his own words, he then "turned the mathematical crank."

In this cosmology, everything in the universe was at one time more densely packed than it is today. The initial structure would have contained a "timeless zone," a shrinking shell where no time elapsed and no particles interacted. On Day 4 of the creation week, a whole universe-worth of matter and energy passed out of the timeless zone and spread out.

The first material to exit the white hole experienced billions of years from its own perspective, and later matter experienced *millions* of years from its perspective. Yet all of this occurred during a brief moment of Earth time. The white hole ended when the timeless zone self-extinguished upon reaching the center of the universe.

WHITE HOLE MODEL CONCERNS

Not all creation scientists ascribe to the white hole model. Some suspect that even a white hole could not bring light from the most distant quasars all the way to Earth in just one day.

THE BIBLE AND COSMOLOGY

There is still much we need to learn about the cosmos, but whatever we think about the universe needs to fit with the Word of the One who created it. Isaiah 40:22 says that God stretches out the heavens, and Isaiah 34:4 says He will one day roll them up like a scroll. Then God will create a new heavens and a new earth where no sin or decay will enter (2 Peter 3:13), and His redeemed people will live there with Him forever.

Our Perfectly Balanced Solar System

Our solar system demonstrates God's ingenuity and design in His creation. It's made up of the sun and all celestial bodies that orbit the sun. This includes the eight planets as well as asteroids (minor planets), comets, centaurs, dwarf planets, trans-Neptunian objects, and even dust. We can actually see much of the solar system from Earth on a cloudless night, especially with the aid of a telescope.

THE SUN

The sun, a sphere of hydrogen and helium gas, makes up 99.8% of all the mass in the solar system. The sun appears small in our sky because it's 93 million miles away from us!

THE EIGHT PLANETS

After the sun, the next largest objects in the solar system are the planets. Jupiter measures significantly larger than the other planets, with a diameter 11 times the size of Earth's. Saturn is the next largest planet, followed by Uranus, Neptune, Earth, Venus, Mars, and Mercury. All eight planets orbit the sun in the same direction (counterclockwise as viewed from Earth's north pole) and are in nearly the same plane. This plane is called the *ecliptic*.

PLANETARY ORBITS

In the 17th century, creation scientist Johannes Kepler discovered that the planets do not move around the sun in perfect circles but in the shape of "squashed" circles called *ellipses*. Scientists refer to this discovery as Kepler's first law of planetary motion. Building on this law, Isaac Newton, a brilliant scientist and Bible scholar, discovered that gravity causes the orbital motions of planets.

Johannes Kepler

TWO TYPES OF PLANETS

The four planets nearest the sun are *terrestrial,* which means "earthlike." Though Earth is the only planet fit for life, all four are relatively small worlds with dense, rocky compositions. In order of increasing distance from the sun, the terrestrial planets are Mercury, Venus, Earth, and Mars.

The four outer planets—Jupiter, Saturn, Uranus, and Neptune—are called *gas giants* or *Jovians,* which means "like Jupiter." Much larger than terrestrials, they are comprised primarily of hydrogen and helium gas instead of rock.

Mercury

Venus

Earth

Mars

Jupiter

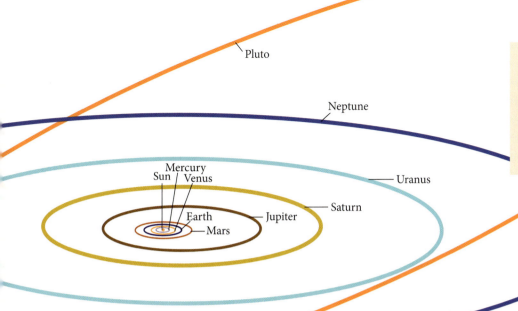

Pluto

Neptune

Mercury
Sun Venus

Uranus

Saturn

Earth
Jupiter

Mars

SOLAR SYSTEM DISTANCES

The vast distances between the planets are difficult to visualize. The University of Colorado has a scale model of the solar system, with the sun represented by a grapefruit-size sphere on a pedestal. Earth is located 50 feet away and is shown at the same scale—a tiny bump about 1/20 of an inch. Mercury, Venus, and Mars sit just a few feet away and are a bit smaller than Earth. Jupiter, considerably farther out, is represented by a marble. To get to Neptune, a person must take a 10-minute walk all the way to the other side of the university campus. The orbits of the outer planets have considerably more space between them than those of the inner planets.

DID YOU KNOW?

The closer a planet is to the sun, the stronger the sun's gravity acts on it and the faster the planet orbits. Mercury travels at over 100,000 miles per hour, but distant Neptune only travels about 12,000 miles per hour. It takes Neptune over 164 years to go around the sun once.

BALANCED BY DESIGN

God created our solar system complete, intact, and perfectly balanced during the creation week just thousands of years ago. We benefit from His perfect design moment by moment, and without it we could not survive. The Bible teaches that God directly controls the universe—that by the word of His power everything is upheld (Hebrews 1:3).

God is not a god of confusion (1 Corinthians 14:33), so He sustains the universe in a consistent and often predictable way. Laws of nature are not a substitute for God's power; rather, they are examples of it. In fact, God's precise sovereignty over the universe is what makes astronomy possible.

Saturn

Uranus

Neptune

The Sun: Supporting Life on Earth

Our sun is a main-sequence star that sends out more energy every second than a billion cities would use in a year. Its composition resembles that of other stars, and its temperature and brightness measure in the average range. This may make its existence seem common and ordinary, but our sun is actually a gracious gift. Many unique and special features show that our Creator clearly designed it to support our lives here on Earth.

"Then God made two great lights: the greater light to rule the day, and the lesser light to rule the night." (Genesis 1:16)

DID YOU KNOW?

Nuclear fusion gradually changes a star's core density, causing it to brighten over time. So if the sun were billions of years old, it would've been about 30% dimmer in the distant past. With less heat reaching Earth, our planet would be a frozen wasteland and life would be impossible!

SIZE AND LOCATION

At 93 million miles away, our sun sits at the heart of the solar system and appears to us as a very small sphere in our sky. But appearances can be deceiving. It actually measures 109 times the diameter of Earth and over a million times Earth's volume.

DID YOU KNOW?

The sun comprises 99.8% of the solar system's mass. If a 10-pound bowling ball represented the mass of the sun, then all the planets, moons, comets, and asteroids could be represented by one nickel and one penny. Jupiter would be the nickel.

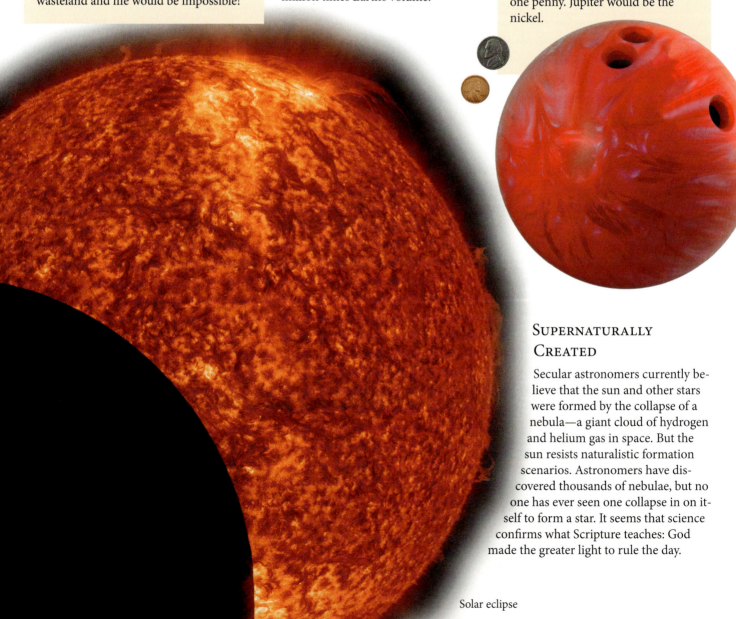

SUPERNATURALLY CREATED

Secular astronomers currently believe that the sun and other stars were formed by the collapse of a nebula—a giant cloud of hydrogen and helium gas in space. But the sun resists naturalistic formation scenarios. Astronomers have discovered thousands of nebulae, but no one has ever seen one collapse in on itself to form a star. It seems that science confirms what Scripture teaches: God made the greater light to rule the day.

Solar eclipse

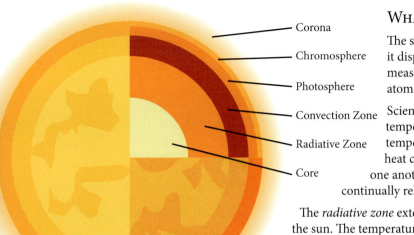

- Corona
- Chromosphere
- Photosphere
- Convection Zone
- Radiative Zone
- Core

What Is the Sun Made of?

The sun is made almost entirely of hydrogen and helium gas, yet it displays remarkable complexity. Using a spectroscope, which measures certain properties of light, we can analyze the sun's atomic fingerprint.

Scientists categorize the sun's layers by their variations in temperature and motion. The *core* is the hottest region, with temperatures exceeding 15 million degrees Celsius. Such high heat causes the protons from the hydrogen atoms to smash into one another and form helium. This process, called *nuclear fusion*, continually releases an enormous amount of energy.

The *radiative zone* extends outside the core to about two-thirds the radius of the sun. The temperature in this region is still millions of degrees, but it's not hot enough for nuclear fusion.

The *convection zone* is the outermost third of the sun where the ionized gas moves in large overturning cells. This layer rotates differentially—the equatorial regions rotate faster than the polar regions. So the outer third of the sun constantly twists itself up. Scientists think this twisting contributes to the reversal of the sun's global magnetic field every 11 years.

The *photosphere*—the visible surface of the sun—encases the convection zone and has a temperature of about 6,000 degrees Celsius. It also has small darker regions called *sunspots*. Magnetic fields inhibit convection and prevent the layer below from transporting energy into these regions. This makes the sunspots cooler and darker than the surrounding areas. The number of sunspots grows and fades in an 11-year cycle and correlates to the reversal of the global magnetic field.

The nearly transparent *chromosphere* surrounds the photosphere. "Chromo" means "color." The gases in the chromosphere have very low density, which makes them invisible under normal circumstances. Only during a total solar eclipse, at the instant of totality when the moon blocks the brighter photosphere, can we see the colorful ring of the chromosphere.

A circle of extremely thin ionized gas called the *corona* envelopes the chromosphere. "Corona" means "crown." The name fits well since this layer surrounds the visible disk of the sun.

Did you know?

The sun contains such high temperatures on the inside that its atoms are completely ionized—meaning their electrons have been stripped away from their nuclei.

Designed for Life

The position of the sun seems optimized for life. If the sun were positioned much closer to Earth, we'd burn up. If it were farther away, we'd freeze like popsicles. And if it were close to the Milky Way's galactic core, the radiation from other stars could harm life on Earth.

Stars hotter than our sun produce far more ultraviolet radiation that would have damaging effects on living tissue. Cooler stars emit far more infrared "heat" for a given amount of visible light. Some stars have superflares that release deadly radiation, but our sun's flares are mild. Thankfully, our sun's temperature, location, and stability fall into the perfect range for life on Earth. God gave us a star that suits us just right.

Melting on Mercury

The planet Mercury could boast many claims to fame—it's the smallest, the quickest, and most elliptical in its orbit of any planet in the solar system. It also travels closest to the sun, making it a scorching-hot place to visit during the day. Mountains, valleys, plains, and lots of craters cover its rocky surface, so you might mistake this planet for a slightly larger version of our moon.

MERCURY'S YEAR

Since it's so close to the sun, Mercury's "year" measures the shortest of any solar system planet—only 88 Earth days long! That means Mercury orbits the sun four times while Earth orbits only once.

A REALLY LONG DAY

Though Mercury has the shortest year, it ironically has the longest solar day. An observer on this planet would only see the sun rise every 176 Earth days! Mercury orbits the sun at a blazing 100,000 miles per hour and rotates only slightly fast enough to overcome this movement to produce an occasional sunrise and sunset.

Mercury

800°

EXTREME TEMPERATURES

Mercury orbits three times closer to the sun than Earth does, and it has very little atmospheric protection. So its long days cause some pretty extreme temperatures. When the sun shines on the rocky planet's surface, its temperature can reach 800 degrees Fahrenheit. But the lack of atmosphere allows this heat to quickly escape after sunset, causing the surface temperature to plummet beneath -280 degrees during the night. Obviously, these extremes make Mercury completely unsuitable for life.

-280°

DID YOU KNOW?

We can't credit a particular person for discovering Mercury since many can spot it from Earth without a telescope, and even ancient cultures knew of its existence.

MAGNETIC FIELD: PROOF OF YOUTH

In 1974, NASA sent the *Mariner 10* spacecraft to Mercury, and it detected a magnetic field—a problem for secular scientists. If the solar system were truly billions of years old, Mercury's magnetic field would have decayed by now. Its presence strongly indicates youth.

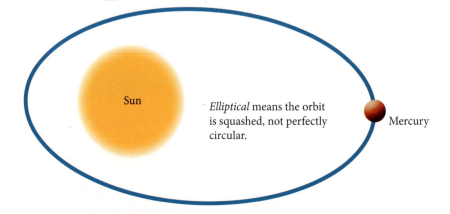

Sun

Elliptical means the orbit is squashed, not perfectly circular.

Mercury

FINDING MERCURY IN THE SKY

We can't view Mercury late at night since we would be looking away from the sun and Mercury orbits closer to the sun than Earth. However, finding it in the daytime can be difficult since it often gets lost in the sun's glare. It's best to search for Mercury at twilight during times of the year when it appears most distant from the sun—a position in orbit called *greatest elongation*. Since Mercury orbits so quickly, it reaches greatest elongation six or seven times during our year, providing us with numerous opportunities to see it.

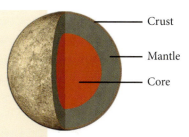

DID YOU KNOW?

Only 25% of Mercury's radius is rock. Most of its interior is made of metallic material

- Crust
- Mantle
- Core

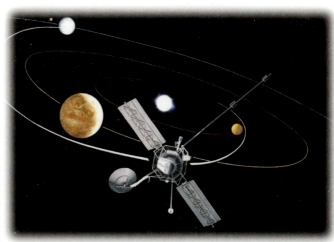

Mariner 10

Messenger

MISSIONS TO MERCURY

In 1974, *Mariner 10* completed the first mission to Mercury. NASA's goal for this mission was to study the atmosphere (if any), surface, and physical characteristics of the rocky planet. This mission was the first time a spacecraft used one planet's gravity to slingshot to another. *Mariner* used the gravity of Venus to slingshot over to Mercury. It flew by Mercury three times before running out of fuel and sent back groundbreaking information on the planet's magnetic field and surface features. The *Messenger* spacecraft, which visited Mercury starting in 2011, orbited for four years, then ran out of fuel and crashed on the planet's rocky surface.

CRATERS: CLUES TO THE PAST?

Creationists have long debated when and how craters in our solar system actually formed. Were the planets created with craters? Did they happen after the Curse or during the Flood year? If so, why? Most other rocky worlds in our solar system have tectonic, atmospheric, and volcanic activity that can erase evidence of previous craters—but not Mercury. Its surface may be a window into the original conditions of our solar system.

Venus, Earth's Sister Planet

As the "evening star," Venus outshines all the stars and planets in the western night sky. Sometimes it appears just before sunrise in the eastern sky as the bright "morning star." Ancient astronomers named Venus after the Roman goddess of love and beauty.

But Venus isn't a star, it's a planet—the second planet from the sun in our solar system and a rocky world that shines by reflected sunlight. Thick, swirling clouds of sulfuric acid and toxic sulfur dioxide continually shroud its surface, masking all its features. Its atmosphere, comprised mainly of carbon dioxide, is the thickest of the four terrestrial planets. This gives Venus a crushing atmospheric pressure 92 times greater than Earth's!

SCORCHING TEMPERATURES

Venus orbits 26 million miles closer to the sun than Earth does, so it endures nearly twice the solar energy. The thick atmosphere acts like a blanket, trapping heat and warming the planet to extreme temperatures. This greenhouse effect causes the surface temperature to approach 900 degrees Fahrenheit—the hottest of any planet in our solar system! You may want to choose a different destination for your summer vacation.

What does Venus look like beneath the blanket of clouds? Check out this radar image of its dramatic rocky surface.

DID YOU KNOW?

Venus has no rings or moons.

Thick clouds always cover Venus—this is the view we see with a telescope.

DAYS AND YEARS

Venus exhibits the most circular orbit of any planet in the solar system. Its axial tilt is only three degrees—compared to the Earth's 23.5 degrees—so Venus has no seasons. Since it orbits faster and closer to the sun than Earth, it only takes 7.4 months to complete one revolution. But Venus rotates only once every eight months, so its day is actually longer than its year!

A three-dimensional, computer-generated image of Venus' giant volcano Maat Mons

Bright Venus looks a lot like a star.

FINDING VENUS

Venus serves as a great target for beginning stargazers. Its brightness makes it easy to find through even a small telescope. Observers will immediately notice that this planet has phases much like the moon; it's not uniformly illuminated but appears bright on one side and dark on the other. Venus goes through new, crescent, quarter, gibbous, and full phases.

BACKWARD ROTATION

Even more intriguing is that Venus rotates *backward*. All eight planets orbit the sun counterclockwise as viewed from the solar system's North Pole. Most of the planets also rotate counterclockwise, but Venus is the exception. On Venus, the sun would rise in the west and set in the east…if you could see it through the thick blanket of clouds.

Secularists don't have a good explanation for this backward rotation. In the secular scenario, the solar system formed from the collapse of a rotating nebula. So, all planets should rotate in the same direction at about the same rate, and all should have very little axial tilt. Venus contradicts this concept since it rotates exactly the opposite of what the evolutionary models require. But we expect such planetary diversity from our Creator!

DID YOU KNOW?

Venus' size and composition are similar to Earth's—both are rocky terrestrial planets—and Venus' orbit is physically closest to Earth's of all the planets. So, Venus is sometimes referred to as Earth's sister or Earth's twin.

VENUS MATCHES THE CHRISTIAN WORLDVIEW

For Venus and Earth to exhibit such similarity in geological features while also possessing many differences is consistent with the nature of God. God created diversity within the universe, and yet similarities abound since the entire universe was created by the same God. We also see differences and similarities in the biological world and the world of particle physics. But how can the secular view make sense of this? Earth and Venus are nearly identical in size and bulk composition and have similar orbits. In the secular view, they should have a similar history, too. So why would Earth's "sister" planet be lifeless and so radically different? Secular scientists can make speculations, but such diversity matches expectations in the Christian worldview.

MAGELLAN'S MISSION

In 1990, the NASA spacecraft *Magellan* orbited Venus while radar-mapping its surface in unprecedented detail. The four-year mission revealed that Venus has many of the same geological features found on Earth—mountains, valleys, canyons, volcanoes, lava flows, craters, and plains. But it has no oceans and no life.

NASA launched the space probe *Magellan* from the *Atlantis* space shuttle in 1989. Also known as the Venus Radar Mapper, it took 15 months to reach Venus.

A SYMBOL FOR CHRIST

Scripture refers to Venus as the "morning star," using its brilliance as a symbol for Christ (Revelation 2:28; 22:16). None of the nighttime stars can compete with bright Venus, so it is a fitting symbol of the beauty and glory of our Lord.

"It is He who sits above the circle of the earth, and its inhabitants are like grasshoppers, who stretches out the heavens like a curtain, and spreads them out like a tent to dwell in." (Isaiah 40:22)

Space Station Flyover of the Mediterranean. Expedition 46 flight engineer Tim Peake of the European Space Agency (ESA) shared this stunning nighttime photograph with his social media followers on January 25, 2016, writing, "Beautiful night pass over Italy, Alps and Mediterranean."

Our Extraordinary Earth

When the *Voyager 1* spacecraft reached the edge of our solar system in 1990, it turned around and photographed Earth. From that distance, Earth appears as a tiny bluish-white grain of sand lost in an ocean of black. This famous image is named the Pale Blue Dot. From a secular perspective, that's all Earth is—a tiny bit of fortunate rock and water in a vast, meaningless cosmos of chance. But in the Christian worldview, Earth is the most important planet in the universe.

The Pale Blue Dot

Did you know?

God provided a special magnetic shield that protects Earth from solar and cosmic radiation. At the same time, visible sunlight must get past this shield to shine on land and sea plants so that light energy can become life energy through photosynthesis. The lifeless too-hot Venus and Mercury and toxic Mars do not have this defensive magnetic shield.

Properties of Earth

Earth orbits the sun at an average distance of 93 million miles, and we refer to this distance as one *astronomical unit*, or AU. At one AU, it takes one year to complete an orbit. Many astronomical measurements are defined in terms of Earth's orbital or rotational characteristics. Earth rotates within 24 hours, the measure of our days. Physically, Earth's properties resemble those of the other terrestrial planets—Mercury, Venus, and Mars. These solid, rocky worlds orbit relatively close to the sun and have mountains, valleys, rifts, canyons, and craters. But despite these similarities, Earth stands out in many ways.

Uniqueness of Earth

So far, all other planets detected by telescopes have proved to be too extreme for life in temperature, gravity, chemistry, and pressure. They also lack liquid water. Even the most Earth-like exoplanet, Kepler 438b, experiences radiation blasts from superflares with a power of 100 billion megatons of TNT. These blasts occur about every few hundred days, making life impossible. So Earth does not represent one insignificant planet in a universe of many others. On the contrary, its unique qualities appear to be specially designed for life to flourish.

WATER

Liquid water covers over 70% of Earth's surface. No other known planet has such an abundance of water. Earth orbits at just the right distance from the sun for temperatures that allow water to remain in liquid form. Atmospheric pressure is also just right for liquid water. Since water is essential for all known life, its presence on Earth represents a key design feature.

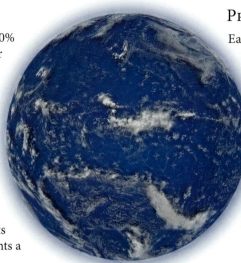

Pacific Ocean

THE MAGNETIC FIELD

The strength of Earth's magnetic field has been continually decreasing since scientists began measuring it nearly two centuries ago. This decay rate agrees with Earth's biblical age of around 6,000 years but cannot be reasonably reconciled with the secular assumption of billions of years. If the earth's magnetic field were more than 50,000 years old, it would have started out so strong it would have been lethal.

PLATE TECTONICS

Earth is the only planet known to have *plate tectonics*. While other planets have volcanoes, their crusts are not divided into movable plates. Many creation scientists believe that Earth's continents were connected before the global Flood and moved apart during the Flood year. A scientific model called *runaway subduction* explains the rapid tectonic plate motions during the Flood that would have caused the continents to break apart and move quickly to their current locations. Noting that rocks begin to behave like thick liquids at high temperatures, the model shows plates sliding during the Flood at meters per minute, not centimeters per year as secular scientists claim.

PROTECTIVE FEATURES

Earth's atmosphere has a protective layer of ozone that partially blocks ultraviolet radiation and a strong magnetic field that deflects harmful cosmic radiation. Without these protective features, life could not exist on Earth.

AN IDEAL TILT

Earth tilts on its axis 23.4 degrees relative to its orbit around the sun. This causes Earth to experience seasons. If it tilted less, the polar regions would receive less energy, reducing the habitable area of our planet. If it tilted more, the seasons would be more extreme, making the environment less hospitable to life.

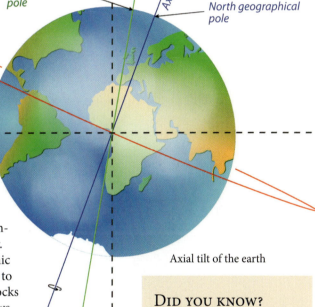

Axial tilt of the earth

DID YOU KNOW?

The ecliptic is the plane of Earth's path around the sun.

GOD'S WORK ON EARTH

Earth is uniquely designed for life. God chose to spend five of the six days of creation working on Earth, making it just the way He wanted it. All the other planets were created in one day—Day 4. It appears God took extra care to create Earth and uniquely designed it to sustain and promote life.

Astronomers have discovered hundreds of planets orbiting other stars, and perhaps countless more remain undiscovered. Yet of all the planets in the universe, Earth is where God chose to place the creatures whom He made in His own image. It is our planet where almighty God, out of His great love for us, took on human nature, paid our death penalty for sin, and rose in glory. Not bad for a pale blue dot!

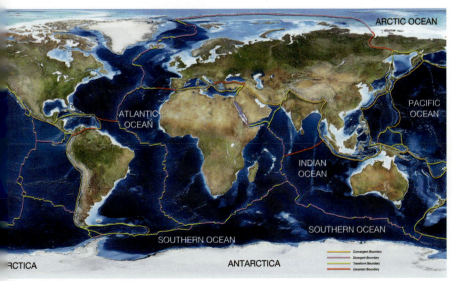

Map of tectonic plates

The Making of the Moon

Then God made two great lights: the greater light to rule the day, and the lesser light to rule the night. (Genesis 1:16)

God gave us the moon for nighttime light. It doesn't shine on its own—it reflects the light it receives from the sun. No other planet has such a bright moon in its night sky, and no other planet has one this large in proportion to the planet's size. The moon is more than a gigantic nightlight—God also made it to support life on Earth.

DID YOU KNOW?

As far as we know, only Earth can experience eclipses in which a planet's moon so precisely covers the sun. Though the sun's diameter is about 400 times larger than that of the moon, it's also 400 times farther away. These proportional differences make them appear to be the same size in our sky.

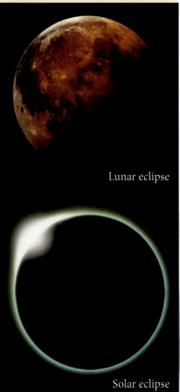

Lunar eclipse

Solar eclipse

AN IDEAL DESIGN

The moon's perfect size and orbit stabilize Earth's tilt, giving us our four seasons and allowing Earth's climate to avoid dangerous variations. Its gravity also induces tides that prevent our oceans from stagnating. Secular scientists claim the moon's existence and ideal traits developed purely by accident. But could chance really produce prime conditions to support life on Earth?

A YOUNG MOON

The moon causes our oceans' tides. Since Earth rotates faster than the moon orbits, the tidal bulges get "ahead" of the moon. This mass of ocean water then pulls forward on the moon so that it gains orbital energy and moves away from Earth about 1.5 inches every year in a process called *recession*. This recession would have been faster in the past because the tides would have been larger when the moon was closer.

If we use this information to calculate the moon's distance from Earth in the past, we find that it would have been touching Earth 1.4 billion years ago. So Earth and the moon cannot be older than that. Yet secular scientists claim that both are over four billion years old.

Six thousand years ago, the moon would have been only 730 feet closer to Earth. So lunar recession does not conflict with the biblical timescale.

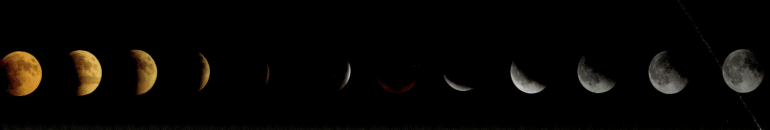

Stages of a lunar eclipse

WHAT IS IT LIKE?

The lunar surface is barren and rocky, with heavily cratered highlands. Lower, smooth regions called *maria* appear as large, dark regions we can see from Earth. These are impact basins that have filled in with magma, erasing previous craters.

The moon has no substantial atmosphere. Its sky remains black even when the sun is up, and surface temperatures can exceed 200 degrees Fahrenheit during the day and drop to -280 degrees Fahrenheit at night.

TIDAL LOCKING

Some people think the moon doesn't rotate since we always see the same side, but this isn't so. The moon takes 27.3 days to rotate once—exactly the time it takes to orbit Earth. For this reason, observers on Earth only see one side of it. If the moon didn't rotate relative to the stars, we would see different sides as it orbits Earth. The fact that its rotation and revolution have exactly the same period is called *tidal locking*. All large and many small moons in our solar system are tidally locked.

DID YOU KNOW?

Maria is Latin for "seas."

SECULAR ORIGIN THEORIES

Where did the moon come from? According to secularists, it formed when a Mars-size object struck Earth long ago. Rocky debris from this cosmic collision supposedly came together and formed the moon we see today and launched it into its perfect orbit.

No part of this scenario was ever observed, and moon experts don't agree on its particulars. If secular scientists don't know the origin of the moon—our closest celestial neighbor—then it would be reasonable to question their explanations for the origins of anything else in the universe.

"For by Him all things were created that are in heaven and that are on earth, visible and invisible, whether thrones or dominions or principalities or powers. All things were created through Him and for Him. And He is before all things, and in Him all things consist." (Colossians 1:16-17)

Earthrise — view of Earth from the moon

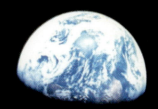

Mysterious Mars

Meet Mars, the most Earth-like planet in our solar system. It's a rocky world about half the size of Earth in diameter. Nicknamed the Red Planet, Mars' surface mostly contains oxidized compounds of iron—better known as rust. Its similarities to Earth make it a tempting target for space colonization, but its stark differences provide many obstacles to that goal.

GEOLOGY

Geologically, Mars has features like those on Earth—mountains, canyons, volcanoes, and even polar ice caps. It also has seasons, clouds, fog, wind, dust storms, and frost. Although liquid water is scarce, scientists discovered water ice near the poles and some water vapor in the Martian atmosphere.

A MARTIAN DAY

Mars takes 24 hours and 37 minutes to rotate once on its axis—almost identical to Earth. The sun appears smaller than it does on Earth and shines at only half the brightness since Mars orbits farther from the sun.

BLUE SKY

In the daytime, Mars' sky is bright, though not as bright as ours. It's often blue for the same reason Earth's sky is blue: the molecules in its thin atmosphere scatter shorter blue wavelengths more readily than longer red wavelengths.

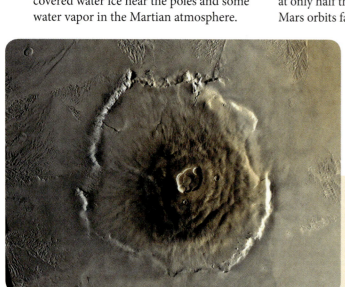

DID YOU KNOW?

Mars' Olympus Mons volcano stands taller than Earth's Mt. Everest.

Olympus Mons

ATMOSPHERE AND GRAVITY

With a thin, mainly carbon dioxide atmosphere, Mars doesn't have a breathable environment. To visit, future astronauts would need spacesuits with oxygen supplies and the atmospheric pressure and temperature necessary for humans. Because its gravity is only 38% of that on Earth, walking on Mars would take practice. By comparison, the moon's gravity is only 17% of Earth's.

LANDSCAPE

Mars' surface resembles Earth's deserts. It has hills and even enormous mountains, but their gentle slopes make them seem less dramatic than peaks on Earth. Olympus Mons is an extinct volcano—the largest one known—and it stands nearly three times as tall as Mt. Everest.

TILT, ORBIT, AND SEASONS

With an axial tilt of 25.2 degrees, Mars experiences four seasons. But its orbit is significantly more elliptical than Earth's, which causes its distance from the sun to vary more. This makes the seasons more severe in its southern hemisphere. Mars' polar ice caps grow during the winter in their respective hemispheres and shrink during the summer—just like the ice caps on Earth.

Valles Marineris

VALLES MARINERIS

One of Mars' most spectacular features is the Valles Marineris, a canyon long enough to span the entire United States. It measures about 2,500 miles long, 120 miles wide, and four miles deep. This is nearly 10 times longer, seven times wider, and four times deeper than Grand Canyon! Valles Marineris is likely a tectonic fissure—a place where the surface cracked open.

DID YOU KNOW?

One Martian year equals 1.9 Earth years.

A MARTIAN FLOOD?

Mars' surface has dry riverbeds and deltas. Though liquid water has not been seen on the planet today, its erosion features suggest that it once had lots of surface water. This is surprising in light of the planet's thin atmosphere. Water can only exist as a liquid between certain temperatures and under sufficient atmospheric pressure. The atmosphere of Mars is far too thin to allow water to be liquid for any length of time at any temperature.

So, was the Martian atmosphere different in the past? Or was the water released catastrophically, boiling away almost immediately? These mysteries remain unsolved. Strangely, secularists are willing to believe in catastrophic, planet-scale flooding on Mars—a planet that cannot currently support liquid water. Yet they simultaneously deny the Genesis Flood on Earth—a planet that is 71% covered with water.

MARTIAN MOONS

Mars' two moons are tiny compared to Earth's moon. Phobos measures about 10 miles in diameter, and Deimos is only eight miles. More like two large boulders orbiting Mars, neither Phobos nor Deimos is spherical.

From a secular perspective, the origin of these moons is difficult to explain. Were they once asteroids that have since been "captured" by the gravity of Mars? It's possible but involves an improbable chain of events. And captured asteroids are expected to have exaggerated, elliptical orbits, but Mars' moons orbit in nearly perfect circles.

Phobos

Deimos

Mars

CLEARLY SEEN

Mars and Earth possess great similarities but also vast differences. This is yet one more mark of the creativity of the God of Scripture. The evidence of Him is clearly seen by what He has made—"even His eternal power and Godhead" (Romans 1:20).

Perhaps one day there will be an astronaut walking on Mars—maybe it will be you!

Spirit of St. Louis Crater (below), taken by the panoramic camera on the Mars Exploration Rover *Opportunity* in March 2015.

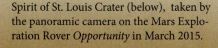

43

rating Saturn

If Saturn competed in a solar system beauty pageant, it would take home the crown. Though it is nine times the size of Earth, it possesses the lowest density of any solar system planet and is encircled by many beautiful rings of ice. Hydrogen and helium gas make up this sixth planet from the sun, and remnants of methane and ammonia give it a sandy, yellowish hue. It takes 29.5 years for Saturn to complete just one orbit.

RINGS OF ICE

Admirers of Saturn often favor the planet for its delicate icy rings. Thankfully, Saturn's axis tilts just right to grant us a perfect view of them throughout most of the year. Without the right tilt, the rings would be rendered almost invisible because we would barely get a peek at their ultra-thin edges. Though the rings span 170,000 miles across, they are surprisingly only one mile thick.

DID YOU KNOW?

We get to see Saturn from a variety of angles as it orbits the sun. The best view of its rings comes during Saturn's summer and winter solstices, when the sun shines farthest from Saturn's equator.

THEY SHINE LIKE NEW

Saturn's rings testify to a young universe. The ice still appears bright and shiny and lacks the thick layer of space dust that should have collected on its surface if it were as old as secularists say. If the rings were millions of years old, they would display a color closer to that of old, dingy socks. To explain how the rings could still be bright after so much time, secularists have formed a theory that the ring particles collide, fragment, and then re-clump. But scientists have no idea how clumping could occur. And even if it did, the chain of events required would cause some of the rings to merge into each other. Merged rings around Saturn have never been observed.

Saturn's rings face ongoing destructive forces such as plasma drag from Saturn's atmosphere, sunlight pressure, collisional spreading, meteorite impacts, and sputtering (collisions at the atomic level). They would have been destroyed by now had they endured billions of years of these relentless onslaughts.

DID YOU KNOW?

In 2006, NASA reported observations that Saturn's rings are spreading, and the rate of spread does not match the secular ages assigned to Saturn. The report also indicated that Saturn's moons have a short life expectancy because they are being chipped away and churned up into debris so fast that their very presence is a mystery for secular scientists.

TITAN

Saturn has 62 known moons. This count does not include the little moonlets tucked within the planet's rings. Saturn's largest moon, Titan, is the second-largest moon in the solar system, only surpassed by Jupiter's Ganymede, and it is one-and-a-half times the size of our moon. It can be seen through a small telescope or powerful binoculars and looks like an orange star floating next to the planet.

Titan

AURORAS AND THE MAGNETIC FIELD

Like Earth, Saturn offers a broad display of auroras produced by its magnetic field. Auroras are colorful phenomena that stretch across the sky like streamers, typically at the northern or southern poles. They are caused when charged solar particles bombard the upper atmosphere. The Hubble Space Telescope has captured Saturn's auroras in great detail.

Magnetic fields are caused by electrical currents that eventually run out of charge over time. This is similar to what happens with batteries if you leave your flashlight on for too long. Scientific calculations cannot explain how Saturn—or any planet, for that matter—could have existed for billions of years without losing its magnetic field long ago.

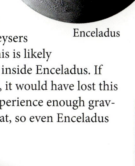
Enceladus

ENCELADUS

Enceladus, another of Saturn's moons, has small craters and a pale white complexion. The 2005 flybys of the *Cassini* spacecraft revealed that an icy substance shoots like geysers out of this moon's southern pole. This is likely due to high temperatures welling up inside Enceladus. If Enceladus were millions of years old, it would have lost this internal heat long ago. It does not experience enough gravitational pull to renew its internal heat, so even Enceladus looks like a recent creation.

Geysers on Enceladus

Saturn's auroras

Unexpected Uranus

Sir William Herschel, a skilled astronomer born in the 1700s, constructed various telescopes and cataloged thousands of distant objects. In fact, his survey formed the basis for the New General Catalogue (NGC) of deep-sky objects still used today.

In 1781, Herschel observed a small blue disk and assumed it was a comet. But as he tracked the object, he found it didn't move like one. Comets generally have highly elliptical orbits, but the orbit of this blue disk was nearly circular. It had to be a planet. Later named Uranus (YOOR-un-us) after the Greek god of the sky, the blue planet was the farthest known object in the solar system at that time.

RECOGNIZING URANUS

Though Herschel identified Uranus as a planet, he wasn't necessarily the first person to see it. Observers can see Uranus with the unaided eye—but just barely. It's likely that ancient astronomers saw it but failed to notice its slow movement relative to thousands of brighter stars.

LOCATION, SIZE, AND COMPOSITION

Uranus orbits the sun at an average distance of 1.79 billion miles—over 19 times farther out than Earth. At four times Earth's diameter, its outer composition is similar to Jupiter's and Saturn's—mostly hydrogen and helium gas. Astronomers believe the interior of Uranus is composed of various ices such as water, ammonia, and methane.

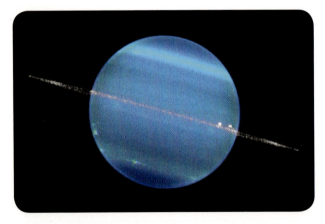

This image of Uranus involves two types of infrared light— which is invisible to human eyes—and uses artificial color to show the details in the planet's surface and rings.

Beneath Uranus' thick, baby-blue atmosphere lies an icy planet.

VOYAGER 2 DISCOVERIES

The *Voyager 2* spacecraft provided the most detailed images to date when it flew past Uranus in 1986. The mission returned pictures of a nearly featureless blue sphere.

Uranus has a system of rings like Saturn, but they are structured very differently. While Saturn's rings are broad sheets of orbiting material, Uranus' rings are more like a series of 13 thin, detached ropes. All encircle the blue planet in the plane of its equator.

DID YOU KNOW?

Uranus is so far away that it takes 84 years to orbit the sun just once.

COUNTERING THE SECULAR MODEL

Unlike any other planet, Uranus rotates on its side—the rotation axis is tilted approximately 90 degrees relative to the planet's track around the sun. Since the rings orbit Uranus' equator, they too are sideways, as are most of its moons. The planet's extreme tilt counters the secular model of solar system formation. Under this model, the planets ought to have formed so that their rotation axis is nearly perpendicular to their orbital plane. Only Jupiter and Mercury meet this expectation.

MAGNETIC RIDDLES

Most planets have a magnetic field that basically aligns with their rotation axis. But Uranus' magnetic axis is offset from the rotation axis by an astonishing 60 degrees. From a secular perspective, Uranus shouldn't have a magnetic field at all. Magnetic fields naturally decay with time and should no longer exist in planets that are billions of years old.

But a strong magnetic field fits perfectly with biblical creation. In 1984, creation physicist Russell Humphreys predicted Uranus' magnetic field strength based on the amount of magnetic decay that would have happened in the 6,000 years since its creation. *Voyager 2* confirmed this prediction.

RECENT CREATION VS. SECULAR EXPLANATIONS

Secular scientists must explain why quickly decaying magnetic fields like Uranus' still exist after billions of years. So, they propose that mechanical motion due to heat in a planet's interior somehow recharges the magnetic field. But of the four giant planets in our solar system, Uranus is the only one without any measurable internal heat. It has no power source for this proposed recharge. Recent creation better explains the remaining strength of magnetic fields.

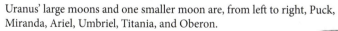

Uranus' large moons and one smaller moon are, from left to right, Puck, Miranda, Ariel, Umbriel, Titania, and Oberon.

MOONS

Twenty-seven known moons orbit Uranus. Oberon and Titania measure the largest. Next are Ariel, Umbriel, and little Miranda. These five major moons can all be seen in a backyard telescope under very dark skies, though viewing Miranda is particularly challenging. The remaining 22 moons are much smaller—less than about 50 miles in radius.

Miranda

A PLANET OF SURPRISES

It's rare for anyone to say Uranus is their favorite planet—it doesn't get a lot of attention. But when we take time to study God's creation, we realize that even the most obscure parts of the universe contain unexpected mysteries and demonstrations of His power and creativity.

Neptune, Blue as the Sea

Over 30 times farther from the sun than Earth, Neptune is the most distant planet in our solar system. Yet it's visible with a backyard telescope. In fact, the famed astronomer Galileo Galilei probably saw Neptune hundreds of years before its official discovery, though he couldn't have distinguished it from the stars. Today we can only see it as a tiny blue sphere in even the most powerful Earth-based telescopes.

A MATHEMATICAL MYSTERY

Scientists discovered Neptune using mathematics before they ever recognized it through a telescope. In the 17th century, creation scientist Sir Isaac Newton mathematically demonstrated that the sun's gravity impacts planetary motion by deflecting the planets' momentum into an elliptical path. This new understanding allowed astronomers to refine their orbit calculations to include the influence of other planets' gravity as well. Using this technique, they predicted the precise position of every known planet except Uranus.

Scientists knew Uranus' orbital path, but its route didn't quite fit the mathematical calculations—even when they factored in the gravitational effects of the other known planets. Was an unknown planet pulling on Uranus?

Urbain Le Verrier

Johann Galle

Sir Isaac Newton

A view of Neptune as it would look from a spacecraft approaching its moon Triton

FINDING NEPTUNE

Urbain Le Verrier, a French mathematician, computed the position that the unknown planet must have in order to explain Uranus' orbit. He mailed his findings to Johann Galle of the Berlin Observatory, who received the letter on September 23, 1846, and viewed Neptune in the sky that very evening. The distant planet stood within one degree of the position Le Verrier had predicted. Le Verrier named his discovery Neptune after the Roman god of the sea and became known as the man who "discovered a planet with the point of his pen."

DID YOU KNOW?

It takes Neptune 164.8 years to orbit the sun one time!

VOYAGER 2

Voyager 2 finally reached Neptune in 1989. Since its launch in 1977, the spacecraft had already visited Jupiter, Saturn, and Uranus. A rare alignment of the outer four planets made this trip possible because NASA scientists could use the gravity of each planet to "slingshot" the craft to the next. *Voyager 2* traveled over four billion miles and became the only spacecraft to visit distant Neptune.

DID YOU KNOW?

Neptune's magnetic field is similar in strength to Uranus'. This is consistent with their biblical age of about 6,000 years but far stronger than what we would expect if the planets were billions of years old. Magnetic fields decay too quickly to last so long.

THE BLUE TWIN

Neptune appears very similar to Uranus—they're practically twins. Both worlds are four Earth-diameters in size and have an icy core surrounded by a thick atmosphere of hydrogen, helium, and small amounts of methane. The methane causes the planets' blue color.

Earth

Neptune

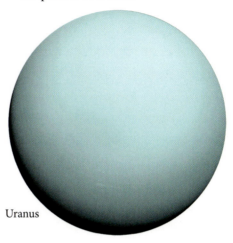

Uranus

Triton

DID YOU KNOW?

Neptune's largest moon, Triton, has a retrograde orbit. This means that, unlike other large moons, it orbits opposite the direction that the planet spins.

VISITING NEPTUNE

Our understanding of Neptune took a leap forward with the *Voyager 2* visit. This exploration revealed a system of rings wrapped around the blue planet that could not be discerned through an Earth-based telescope. At first the rings appeared only as arcs, but as *Voyager 2* drew closer, the five major rings were found to be complete.

The spacecraft also discovered five new moons orbiting close to Neptune, bringing the blue planet's total known moons to eight. Since then, astronomers have discovered six more moons.

Neptune surprised scientists with a large dark spot in its southern hemisphere. It was an Earth-size anticyclone similar to Jupiter's Great Red Spot. Though Jupiter's storm continues to rage, Neptune's died out. In 1994, the Hubble Space Telescope revealed that the southern spot had disappeared, and a new dark spot formed in Neptune's northern hemisphere.

Voyager 2 examined Neptune's moon Triton in superb detail. When the sun heats Triton's frozen surface, it creates "geysers" of nitrogen gas that pick up dark surface dust and launch it into Triton's nitrogen atmosphere. Winds carry the dust many miles, stretching numerous horizontal dark streaks across its southern hemisphere.

CONFIRMATION OF CREATION

Neptune has considerable internal heat, radiating more than twice the energy it receives from the sun. If Neptune were billions of years old, it would have long since run out of this excessive energy. But it makes perfect sense for the planet to still have internal heat with a 6,000-year biblical timescale.

It's interesting that Uranus lacks any internal heat, despite being nearly identical to Neptune in every other way. How can a naturalistic scenario make sense of this? Yet this similarity-with-differences is a common characteristic the Lord built into the universe. Diversity with unity is part of what makes science possible and is what we expect from God.

Neptune's Great Dark Spot

Pluto, the Dwarf Planet

In 1930, astronomer Clyde Tombaugh observed a faint point of light orbiting the sun beyond Neptune. Upon closer examination, this spot of light turned out to be an icy, rocky world reflecting the sun's rays. Eventually named Pluto, it was recognized as the ninth planet in the solar system.

Pluto's classification has been disputed over the last few decades. Whether it's referred to as a planet, a dwarf planet, or a trans-Neptunian object, we know much more about it now thanks to the 2015 images captured by the *New Horizons* spacecraft.

What Is Pluto Like?

Pluto is a small world composed of rock and various types of ice. It has a tilt of 120 degrees and rotates on its side like Uranus. Its average distance from the sun is 3.6 billion miles—39 times Earth's distance. So, it takes Pluto 248 years to orbit the sun just once. On Pluto, the sun would appear over 1,500 times fainter than it does to us, therefore it receives much less of the sun's heat. Its surface temperature hovers at -229 degrees Celsius.

Did you know?

Astronomers who thought they detected Pluto's existence because of gravitational pull were actually mistaken. Pluto is too small to have any significant gravitational pull on the other planets. It was discovered only because astronomers happened to be searching the right spot in the sky.

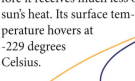
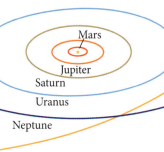

Mars
Jupiter
Saturn
Uranus
Neptune
Pluto

Orbiting by Design

Pluto doesn't orbit the sun within the same plane of the other planets. Its orbit inclines at a 17 degree angle compared to the rest of the solar system planets. Pluto's orbit also has high eccentricity, meaning that its elliptical shape appears very "squashed."

For every three times that Neptune orbits the sun, Pluto goes around twice. Such a stable configuration guarantees that these two worlds can never collide. Could this be an original design feature?

Pluto's Moons

Pluto has five known moons. Charon is the largest, and it's tidally locked. This means it keeps the same side pointed toward Pluto as it revolves. Amazingly, Pluto is also tidally locked with Charon. Pluto's other four moons—Styx, Nix, Kerberos, and Hydra—measure less than 100 miles in diameter.

Did you know?

Hundreds of icy objects in our solar system orbit beyond Neptune.

Charon

Did you know?

Pluto is so far away that even the best pictures taken by the powerful Hubble Space Telescope are fuzzy.

FINDING PLUTO

Neptune's discovery was a triumph of Newtonian physics. The planet was detected not by sight but by its gravitational influence on Uranus' orbit. Some astronomers thought they detected signs of gravitational pull from another planet near Uranus and Neptune that was yet to be discovered. In 1906, Percival Lowell began a search for this undiscovered world he termed "Planet X." He died before finding it.

Clyde Tombaugh resumed the search in 1929. He photographed sections of the sky at different times. Since planets orbit the sun, while stars do not, Planet X would be in a different position on two photographs taken on different nights. Tombaugh used a *blink comparator* that allows a view of two photographic plates in rapid succession. When shifting from one photograph to a nearly identical one, the human brain perceives any change. A planet would appear to jump back and forth when the plates were flipped, while the stars remained stationary. Tombaugh found Planet X, Pluto, by "blinking" between two photographs taken a few days apart.

Percival Lowell (above)
Clyde Tombaugh (left) with his homemade telescope

RECLASSIFYING PLUTO

Before Pluto's discovery, our solar system was divided into the four terrestrial planets that orbit close to the sun and the four gas giants farther out. Pluto broke the mold as a small rocky body at a tremendous distance.

We now know that Pluto is only 1,430 miles in diameter—about 18% the diameter of Earth. And it has less than 1% of Earth's mass. So, in 2006 the International Astronomical Union voted to reclassify Pluto as a *dwarf planet*.

Trans-Neptunian objects

A YOUNG PLUTO

Pluto has mountains, canyons, and evidence of past volcanic activity, which are strong indicators of internal heat and a young age. If the dwarf planet were billions of years old, the surface might be littered with craters, but there are relatively few, and some regions have none—strong evidence of recent creation.

TNOS AND PLUTO'S DEMOTION

Size is one reason for Pluto's demotion, but it's not the only reason. Astronomers have discovered other objects beyond Neptune that are similar in size and composition to Pluto. With these discoveries, astronomers realized Pluto was not an out-of-place planet but one of the largest members of a new class of objects—*trans-Neptunian objects* (TNOs).

In 2005, astronomers discovered a TNO estimated to be *larger* than Pluto—Eris. Either Eris needed to be the tenth planet or Pluto would have to be demoted. Since Pluto and Eris are far more similar to other TNOs than they are to planets, the astronomers opted to revoke Pluto's status as a planet.

NEW HORIZONS

The *New Horizons* spacecraft launched in 2006 and spent nine years traveling three billion miles to Pluto. It flew by the dwarf planet in 2015, taking some of the detailed pictures shown on these pages. The successful mission rewarded us with the first clear, up-close images of Pluto's surface.

New Horizons

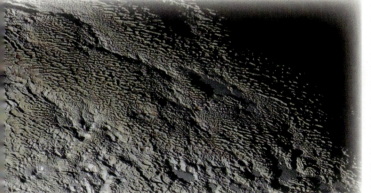

Surface of Pluto

Magnetic Fields and Why They Matter

Have you ever seen the beautiful auroras that stretch across the northern skies of Alaska? These colorful light shows happen when solar wind sufficiently disturbs the magnetic field surrounding Earth. Earth's powerful magnetic field is generated by electrical currents in its metallic core. Without this invisible shield, solar and cosmic radiation would be harmful to life on Earth.

Most magnetic fields—including Earth's—decay quickly, so they can't last for millions of years. Yet we find them still going strong around many planets and moons within our solar system. This challenges secular theories that claim these celestial bodies are millions and even billions of years old.

MERCURY

In 1974 and 1975, the *Mariner 10* spacecraft zipped by Mercury, recording whatever data it could pick up. The spacecraft measured its magnetic field to be about 1% that of Earth's. When *Messenger* returned in 2008, Mercury's field had decayed by 4%. Creation physicist Russell Humphreys accurately predicted the 2008 measurement in 1984 using a Bible-based 6,000-year estimate of the universe's age.

EARTH

Scientists have measured the strength of Earth's magnetic field since 1835. It has decayed about 7% since then. Using this decay rate, we can calculate that the earth's magnetic field has a half-life of around 1,400 years. This means that 1,400 years from now it will be half as strong as it is today. It will be one-fourth as strong 2,800 years from now, and so on. If we calculate backward, we find that 60,000 years ago, the magnetic field would have been as strong as that of a neutron star! Life could not exist. Clearly, Earth is much younger than secularists claim.

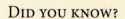

> ### DID YOU KNOW?
> Auroras are mainly visible close to the North and South Poles because the poles' magnetism attracts solar particles when they enter Earth's atmosphere. According to NASA, Alaska, Canada, and Scandinavia are the best locations for viewing auroras.

MOON

The 1969 moon landing allowed us to learn quite a bit about the moon, including its magnetism. Secular scientists have been trying to figure out how the moon could have a magnetic field because according to their models it's too small to have one. Lunar rocks record that the moon's magnetic field was once much stronger, but it has deteriorated and become very faint. If our moon were truly billions of years old, even this remnant of magnetic strength would have disappeared long ago.

NASA astronaut Buzz Aldrin walks on the surface of the moon near the lunar module *Eagle* during the Apollo 11 mission.

JUPITER

Jupiter has the strongest magnetic field of any solar system planet. This kind of magnetic field should have decayed completely if Jupiter has existed for billions of years. But it's still there.

Jupiter

SATURN

In addition to its bright, young-looking rings, Saturn also has a strong magnetic field—578 times more powerful than Earth's! It decays at a rapid rate and could only exist for thousands of years before disappearing. This gives strong evidence of recent creation.

Saturn

URANUS

When *Voyager 2* visited Uranus in 1986, it recorded a magnetic field that was still strong despite the alleged age of billions of years. Russell Humphreys successfully predicted its magnetic strength based on the 6,000-year age indicated by the biblical timescale.

NEPTUNE

When *Voyager 2* visited Neptune in 1989, it recorded a magnetic field comparable to Uranus'. This is far stronger than the secular model predicts, yet Humphreys' model again accurately predicted the amount of decay based on a 6,000-year age.

Voyager 2

DR. RUSSELL HUMPHREYS

Dr. Russell Humphreys is a creation physicist well known for his water origin theory and the successful predictions of magnetic field decay rates. His water origin theory comes from 2 Peter 3:5, which says that the earth in Genesis 1 was "standing out of water and in the water." Humphreys hypothesized that perhaps God made the other planets from water as well. He used this model to successfully predict the magnetic field decays of several planets, including Mercury, Uranus, and Neptune.

THE DYNAMO THEORY

Secular scientists use the dynamo theory to explain how a magnetic field could endure for millions of years. They begin with examples of mechanical energy (motion) being converted into magnetic and electrical energy—like a car's alternator does. They apply these examples to evidence that the earth has reversed polarity throughout history, saying that each reversal (motion) recharged Earth's magnetic field. However, such magnetic reversals have never been shown to recharge a magnetic field.

Studying the Stars

Throughout much of human history, people thought stars were different from the sun. Some believed they were deceased ancestors, angels, or simply luminous points of light on a rotating celestial sphere. Around 450 B.C., Greek philosopher Anaxagoras suggested that the stars were like our sun. The same idea was proposed in 1584 by Italian astronomer Giordano Bruno. Though rejected at the time, this view was later accepted, and now we have a much better understanding of these bright, beautiful celestial bodies that light up our night sky. We know they burn their own fuel, are held together by their own gravity, vary in size and brightness, and display different colors. And as technology advances, we keep learning more.

MAIN SEQUENCE STARS

Most of the stars we observe are main sequence stars. They span from cool red dwarfs—the most numerous kind of stars—to hot blue stars. Technically, any main sequence star is called a *dwarf* regardless of luminosity or temperature, though blue dwarfs are larger than red dwarfs. Our sun is a main sequence yellow dwarf. Though it's a common type of star, the sun is unusually stable. That makes the sun uniquely suited to support life on Earth.

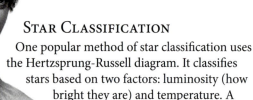

STAR CLASSIFICATION

One popular method of star classification uses the Hertzsprung-Russell diagram. It classifies stars based on two factors: luminosity (how bright they are) and temperature. A star's color is directly related to its temperature. Stars with lower temperatures are red (labeled M), while stars with higher temperatures are blue (labeled O). Main sequence stars follow a common ratio of luminosity and temperature. That is, if it has a certain temperature, then it will be a certain brightness and vice versa.

Giordano Bruno

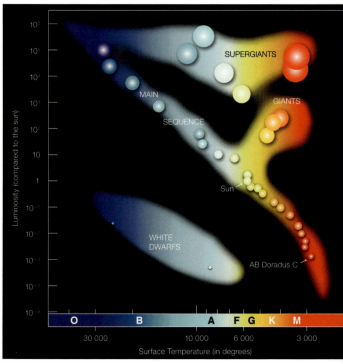

The Hertzsprung-Russell diagram. Credit: ESO

STAR COMPOSITION

Stars burn their own hydrogen fuel through a process called *nuclear fusion* occurring at their centers. The heat of the star's center pushes *out* and its gravity pushes *in*, forming a perfect balance that keeps the star stable. However, when the star runs out of fuel, it collapses. In low-mass stars, this collapse happens slowly, sometimes forming a radiating nebula. For high-mass stars, the collapse happens in a short-lived explosion called a *supernova*.

STAR FORMATION

According to secular scientists, stars form when gases collapse. But this contradicts physics. Gas doesn't naturally compress—it expands. Gas also resists compression because it has a slight magnetic field; its molecules push each other away. The closer they are to each other, the stronger they push. So, trying to form a star by compressing gas is like trying to push the north ends of two magnets together. The laws of magnetism keep star formation from happening.

GIANTS

Giants measure larger than most main sequence stars, and they don't follow the main sequence formula of luminosity and temperature. They typically span a few hundred times bigger than our sun, with luminosities that vary between 10 and a few thousand times greater.

SUPERGIANTS

We call the largest stars *supergiants*. They can be thousands of times larger than our sun, with masses up to 100 times greater. If we were to replace our sun with VY Canis Majoris, one of the largest known supergiants, its edge would touch Saturn.

WHITE DWARFS

White dwarfs are smaller than our sun, but they share a similar mass. A white dwarf is just pressed into a tighter space, making it about one million times denser than our sun. In fact, white dwarfs are the densest objects in the universe outside of black holes and neutron stars. The nearest one we know of is Sirius B, about 8.6 light-years away.

BLACK HOLES

Black holes are legendary enigmas—the stuff science fiction novels are made of. They exhibit such strange characteristics that they seem to defy common sense. For example, all their mass is contained in an incredibly small point at their centers. This causes them to bend space so tightly that even light cannot escape.

The boundary between normal space-time and the point of no return of a black hole's gravitational attraction is called the *event horizon*. Once crossed, no known particle can escape. Scientists think black holes may be the result of massive collapsed stars—big ones like supergiants. They're technically invisible, but we can detect black holes by the movements of surrounding objects like stars and light.

HE MADE THE STARS ALSO

Not only does natural star formation defy the laws of physics, it also defies logic. Every naturalistic theory requires a nearby star to explode and compress gas. So where did the first star come from? The most reasonable conclusion is that God supernaturally created stars in the beginning as the Bible says.

DID YOU KNOW?

Black holes are likely the densest objects in the universe. Some form the center of galaxies, with many stars in orbit.

Blue Stars and Star Formation

In the nighttime winter sky, it's often easy to spot the constellation of hunter Orion holding his sword and shield. The next time you go stargazing, look for the three bright blue stars composing Orion's belt. They represent strong evidence for the biblical timescale.

Most stars generate energy internally through the process of nuclear fusion of hydrogen into helium—an efficient power source. Theoretically, a star like the sun has enough hydrogen fuel to keep burning for about 10 billion years. But that's not the case with blue stars, which are far more massive than our sun. Their sheer size means they have more hydrogen available as fuel. Yet, blue stars are much brighter and hotter than the sun, so they "use up" their fuel much more rapidly. They cannot last billions of years. In fact, at their current rate, the most massive blue stars could not last even one million years before running out of fuel.

If the universe were really 13.8 billion years old, all of the blue stars would have burned out by now. Yet, blue stars abound in every known spiral galaxy. It seems that none of these countless galaxies can be even one million years old! The biblical timescale of a 6,000-year-old universe easily explains the abundance of blue stars we see today.

Orion constellation

SUPERNOVAS

When massive stars self-destruct, they produce a powerful explosion called a *supernova*. It leaves behind a stellar core and expanding debris. A 13.8-billion-year-old universe could fit about 13,800 blue star "lifetimes." If the universe has existed for so long, why don't we see millions of supernova remnants in the sky?

DID YOU KNOW?

Secular scientists label certain areas in the universe as "star-forming regions" or "stellar nurseries," but no one has seen or documented the formation of a new star.

THE ORIGIN OF STARS IS...OTHER STARS?

Secular astronomers now believe that some external force, such as a shockwave from an exploding star, must trigger star formation. But observations confirm that gas clouds expand. They do not appear to collapse into stars. And if you need exploding stars to create stars—where did those exploding stars come from?

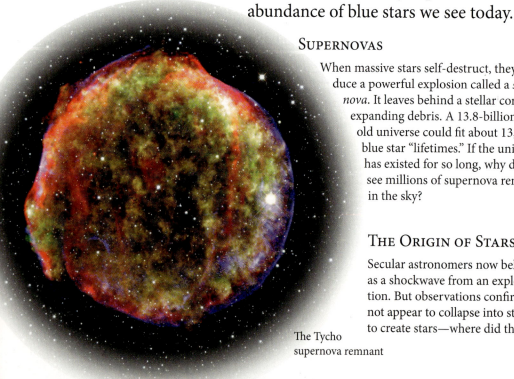

The Tycho
supernova remnant

A Star Is Born—or Is It?

To explain why blue stars still shine, secular astronomers assume that countless new blue stars have formed to replace all those that would have burned out over deep time. They claim that clouds of hydrogen gas called *nebulae* eventually collapse under their own gravity to form new stars. But this is not an observed fact. No one has seen a star form.

Obstacles to Star Formation

Star formation is problematic at best since stars are essentially compressed gas and gas is very resistant to compression. On Earth, gas always fills its container. In space, there is no container, so gas expands almost indefinitely. If the gas in space could be sufficiently compressed and forced into a small sphere such as the sun, then the gas molecules' own gravity would hold them together. However, in a typical nebula, the gas pressure far exceeds the miniscule force of gravity.

> **Did you know?**
> Some blue stars shine 200,000 times brighter than our sun!

Angular Momentum

Gas clouds always have a small amount of angular momentum—they rotate, if ever so slowly. But much like a skater who pulls her arms and legs in as she spins, a collapsing gas cloud would increase its spin rate. The centrifugal force generated would tend to prevent any further collapse. Gas pressure, magnetic field strength, and angular momentum all work to prevent star formation. From a scientific perspective, naturalistic star formation appears quite unlikely.

Supernaturally Created

The star evidence we observe seems far more consistent with the biblical account—it appears that stars were supernaturally created only thousands of years ago. With countless blue stars scattered across the cosmos and very few supernova remnants, our universe certainly appears to be quite young.

Crab Nebula, a supernova remnant

Magnetic Field Strength

Even if we could compress a nebula to the point that the force of gravity was strong enough to prevent the gas from expanding, other effects would kick in to prevent star formation. Clouds of gas always have a weak magnetic field, but it would get much stronger if the cloud were compressed. The magnetic pressure would halt a shrinking cloud and drive it to re-expand. It's a bit like trying to push the like poles of two magnets together.

"When I consider Your heavens, the work of Your fingers, the moon and the stars, which You have ordained, what is man that You are mindful of him, and the son of man that You visit him?" (Psalm 8:3-4)

Stargazing Basics for Beginners

If you're looking for a mind-blowing evening of majestic entertainment for little to no cost, you might consider spending some time *stargazing*. It's easy to get lost in the busyness of life and forget to look up once in a while. But if you take a moment, you might be surprised at the awesome wonders you can see from your own backyard.

CONSTELLATIONS

Constellations can be a lot of fun to spot when you're stargazing. A constellation is a group of stars that form an imaginary picture. People have used constellations to map the stars and mark the changing seasons for thousands of years. A constellation may represent an animal, a mythological creature, a person, or an object.

Astronomers divided the sky into 88 official constellations in 1922. This included the 48 ancient constellations listed by the Greek astronomer Ptolemy. Many more constellations have been named over the years, but these 88 are officially recognized by the International Astronomical Union.

Which constellations are visible to you depends on the hemisphere you live in and what time it is. A sky map can help you locate the constellations in your night sky.

Orion

THE MOVES OF THE MOON

The moon orbits Earth counterclockwise, moving from west to east. But it appears from Earth to move the opposite direction. Why? It's because the moon takes about a month to complete one orbit but the Earth spins *much* more quickly than that. It's like riding in a car and passing a bike. The bike appears to move backward even though it is actually moving forward.

MOONLIGHTING

When the moon is on the opposite side of Earth from the sun, you can fully see its lighted round shape. We call that a *full moon*. When the moon is between the earth and sun and no part of it shines, it's called a *new moon*.

A full moon tends to wash out starlight, so a better time to stargaze is during a new moon. City lights can have a similar effect, so you can see the night sky much better in rural areas.

TRACKING THE MOON'S PHASES

It takes about a week for the moon to pass through one fourth of its cycle, and it transitions like clockwork. If the sun shines on its right side, the moon will shine brighter the next night as it moves toward the full moon phase—a transition known as *waxing*. If it's illuminated on its left side, it'll grow dimmer as it moves toward the new moon—we call this *waning*.

First Quarter

Waxing Gibbous

Waxing Crescent

Full Moon

New Moon

Waning Gibbous

Waning Crescent

Third Quarter

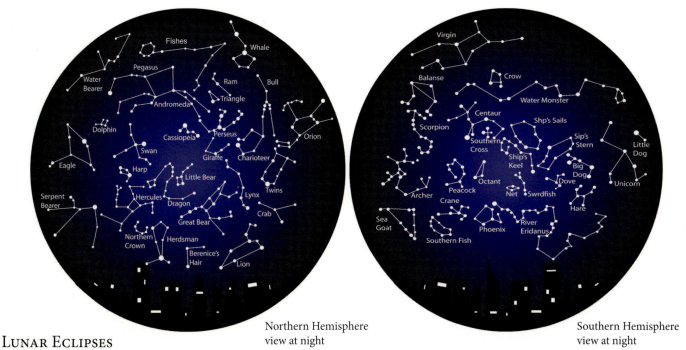

Northern Hemisphere
view at night

Southern Hemisphere
view at night

LUNAR ECLIPSES

A lunar eclipse happens when the earth is positioned exactly between the sun and the full moon. Earth casts its shadow on the moon so that it doesn't receive direct sunlight. Though the moon grows dark during a lunar eclipse, Earth's atmosphere tends to refract sunlight. This bit of indirect light gives the eclipsed moon an orange or reddish glow.

DID YOU KNOW?

Ancient astronomers understood the nature of lunar eclipses well enough to realize that Earth was casting a circular shadow on the moon. The notion that Christopher Columbus was the first to propose that the earth is round and that his journey to America was set to prove it is just a myth.[2]

Comet Hale-Bopp

COMETS

Comets are icy objects that orbit the sun. The sun heats a comet as it draws near, forming a tail that may stretch millions of miles behind it into space. Predicting the motion of comets can be challenging, so it's best to use a computer program or a sky chart in a magazine like *Sky & Telescope*.[3]

DID YOU KNOW?

Meteor showers occur when Earth crosses paths with a comet's debris. The Perseid shower is perhaps the most well known and impressive, raining fire in the night sky from around mid-July to late August.

Starlight and Time

Distant starlight is one of the biggest apparent challenges to biblical history. If the universe is young, how can we see light from a distant star if it has to travel from the farthest reaches of the universe at its measured speed?

Astronomers have detected galaxies several billion light-years away. One light-year—the distance light travels in one calendar year—is about six trillion miles. So has that distant light traveled billions of years to reach Earth today? This would contradict the Bible's record of a universe that's only about 6,000 years old, as well as many scientific measurements that indicate the universe is only thousands of years old. Researchers have offered several possible ways to get distant starlight to Earth in very short times.

BIG BANG LIGHT PROBLEM

Big Bang models suffer from a light-time dilemma of their own called the *horizon problem*, discussed on pages 22-23. Interstellar space temperatures appear to be amazingly consistent in every direction throughout the universe. How did space get such eerily similar temperatures? The regions of space must have exchanged light energy. However, some regions of space lie too far away from stars for enough temperature-leveling light to have reached them, even during the billions of years that Big Bang models assert. Because no Big Bang model has definitively solved the horizon problem, no one can rightly say that it explains the cosmos any better than the Bible does.

THE SHORTCUT

Some think the "shape" of space may be curved, enabling light to take a shortcut through it. In this case, light might take only 15 years to reach Earth from even the farthest known galaxies. However, Genesis 1 suggests that starlight reached Earth on the same day God made stars.

LIGHT SPEED DECAY

Another idea is that the speed of light has decayed. In this scenario, light sped through space much faster long ago and then slowed to today's rate. However, since the forces holding atoms together depend on the speed of light, altering this fundamental rate could have made atoms, and thus all familiar material substances, impossible.

CREATION OF LIGHT BEAMS

When God made stars, did He also create separate light beams connecting them to Earth to allow us to see their distant light? Supernovas give pause to this idea. God would have to embed "movies" that show supernovas inside those light beams, such that the supernova may as well never have actually happened. The supernova "movie" would reach Earth at a certain time after creation. Many think this explanation seems too deceptive for the God of the Bible.

SPEED-OF-LIGHT CONVENTION

Creation astrophysicist Jason Lisle proposed another solution based on Einstein's suggestion that the speed of light in one direction is a human convention, like measuring distance in miles per hour versus kilometers per hour. We can only measure the speed of a light beam *after* it reflects off an object and back toward its source. One can assume the light's outbound speed is equal to its inbound speed and then give that convention any name. Or one can say its outbound speed is half the measured two-way speed as long as its inbound speed is infinite, then call this convention another name. The convention doesn't matter as long as the *round-trip* speed matches about 671 million miles per hour. Instant inbound light speeds would display supernovas in real time, not billions of years after they occurred. This convention would also solve the starlight and time challenge without violating any physical laws.

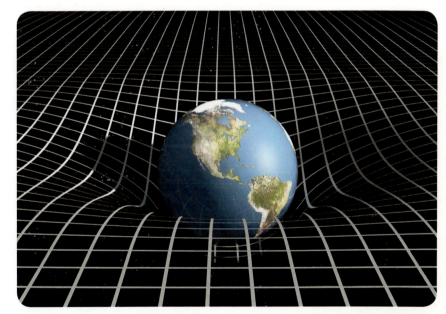

Earth has a gravitational field that affects the space and even the time around it.

MATURE CREATION

On Day 3 of the creation week, God made trees, not just seeds. Ordinarily trees take years to grow, but the Lord performed an extraordinary feat when He made the first trees in no time. Similarly, God may have placed stars at distances so great that light would ordinarily take eons to reach us but used a miracle to accelerate the starlight.

EVERY REASON TO TRUST

Many details about outer space and the nature of light and time still await discovery. More observations promise better answers. Meanwhile, we have every reason to trust that God did just what He said: He created stars on Day 4 to be "lights in the firmament of the heavens to give light on the earth" (Genesis 1:15).

...pace and Other Marvels

64 ...) one of the universe's countless stars and planets shines with a unique light. Each spins in a distinct direction or interacts with unique stellar partners. In fact, the spectacular variety of phenomena that fill the universe is out of place for chance-based, nature-only explanations. But we would expect these artistic wonders based on Scripture: "One star differs from another star in glory" (1 Corinthians 15:41). "I have made the earth, and created man on it. I—My hands—stretched out the heavens" (Isaiah 45:12).

WHAT IS OUTER SPACE?

Outer space describes the area beyond Earth's atmosphere and between celestial bodies. It's almost completely empty, a near-perfect vacuum. This allows planets and moons to orbit freely.

MATURE GALAXIES

Many secular scientists believe that objects found in the most distant reaches of space are billions of years old and should appear far younger than closer objects. But astronomers continually discover fully formed galaxies in locations where they would expect them to be underdeveloped.

The Abell 383 galaxy cluster's gravitational lens enables us to view a galaxy that would ordinarily be too distant for our most powerful telescopes to register. This mature galaxy sits in supposedly immature space. But in reality, every galaxy ever discovered displays completed creation, and no one has observed galaxy formation. This fits well with the Bible's assertion that God recently created space and all its stars, galaxies, and planets—both near and far.

DID YOU KNOW?

Sound can't travel in space because the molecules are too far apart to transmit it. Astronauts must have devices in their helmets that turn sound waves into radio waves so they can hear each other.

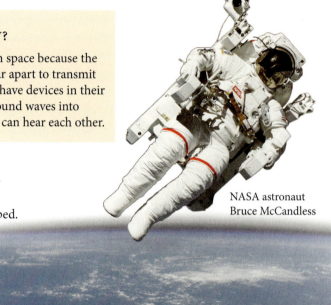

NASA astronaut
Bruce McCandless

QUASARS

Big Bang cosmology assumes matter is distributed evenly throughout the universe and no unique places exist. But neither assumption finds support from observable space features like quasars, which are super-bright, super-massive, quasi-stellar radio sources. Quasars are the brightest objects in the universe, and some of them may contain black holes. A massive network of quasars discovered in 2013 spans a stretch of space four times larger than the maximum "large scale" range that the Big Bang allows. It appears that the whole universe is God's wondrous canvas.

MISSING SUPERNOVA REMNANTS

When a star explodes after burning up its hydrogen fuel, it leaves behind a glowing gas cloud—often a brilliant colorful ring—called a *supernova remnant* or SNR. If the universe is billions of years old, we should see thousands of these remnants, many in the late stages of expansion. Instead, scientists observe only about 200 to 300 visible SNRs and no late-stage ones at all. Not one. According to the number of observed supernova remnants and the rate of supernova occurrences, astronomers estimate that the sky holds only about 7,000 years' worth of supernovas, which compares well with the biblical timescale.

Quasar 3C 273

DID YOU KNOW?

If you picture our solar system as the size of a quarter—the nearest object in the universe would be two soccer fields away!

Crab Nebula

OUT-OF-PLACE STARS

Many stars are binary stars, meaning they are found in pairs that orbit each other. Some pairs with extremely small orbits are orbiting so fast they complete an orbit in less than four hours. This confounds naturalistic scientists. Such a rapid rate of acceleration should take about 28 billion years to build according to their theories, yet they believe the universe is about half that age. If we understand that God put these binary stars in orbit around each other, this rapid speed is no problem.

Stars made almost entirely of hydrogen and helium gas also remain difficult for nature-only advocates to explain. According to their models, stars made of low-mass elements like these should not have been able to condense into a star, especially since they lack heat-dispensing metals.

When all options inside the realm of physics fail to explain a phenomenon, then options outside of physics should be considered. The Word from the One who exists outside of physical space specifically states He made the stars. These stars "declare the glory of God" by confounding man's attempts to replace God with physics (Psalm 19:1).

Asteroids, Comets, and Other Celestial Mysteries

Besides the eight major planets in our solar system, astronomers have observed plenty of minor planets, like asteroids, comets, and centaurs. Just when we think we've discovered it all, we find more celestial objects we didn't even know existed.

> "You are worthy, O Lord, to receive glory and honor and power; for You created all things, and by Your will they exist and were created." (Revelation 4:11)

Discovery of Asteroids

In 1801, Italian astronomer Giuseppe Piazzi was observing the night sky and saw a small planet between the orbits of Mars and Jupiter. He named it Ceres. In the following years, astronomers found more planets in similar orbits, and by the middle of the 19th century they had discovered around 15. They realized they needed a new term for these objects smaller than the eight main planets and called them *asteroids*.

Asteroid Classes

Astronomers categorize asteroids based on their composition or their orbit. Three-quarters of all asteroids are made of carbon (Group C), the second-most common are made of silica (Group S), and the least common are made of metal (Group M). When astronomers categorize asteroids based on their orbits, they get four groups. Most Amor asteroids cross paths with Mars' orbit. The Atira asteroids are entirely inside Earth's orbit, but these are rare—only six have been observed. The Apollo and Aten groups cross Earth's orbit. Orbital categories are named after the first asteroid seen with that path.

Trojan Asteroids

Trojan asteroids share the same orbits as the major planets. They "hide" in the planetary orbits like the ancient Greeks hid in the Trojan horse. Around 6,000 Trojan asteroids have been discovered. Most of them share Jupiter's orbit, so they take just under 12 years to go around the sun, like Jupiter. Other Trojans include four for Mars and one each for Venus, Uranus, and Earth.

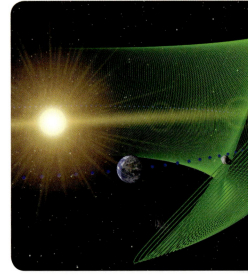

Artist's concept of the first known Earth Trojan asteroid, 2010 TK7

Asteroid Lutetia

Did you know?

Most asteroids disintegrate when they enter Earth's atmosphere. The ones that make it through are small and don't cause much damage. While Earth's orbit does intersect with the orbits of some large asteroids that could cause serious damage, astronomers have calculated their paths and determined that none will hit in our lifetime.

Tycho Brahe

COMETS

In 1577, astronomer Tycho Brahe measured the distance to what was thought to be an atmospheric phenomenon. But he determined that it lay beyond the moon and thus established that comets are celestial objects. Asteroids are mostly rocky, but comets are made of ice and dirt. Their orbits are highly elliptical, meaning they're like a circle that's been really squashed. Comets spend most of their time in the outer solar system beyond Jupiter where they can stay cold, but when they come zipping around the sun they start to vaporize. They can only go around the sun so many times before they completely vaporize.

Comet Hartley 2

COMETS AND CREATION

The creationist worldview is not dependent upon these hypotheses. Comets *can* easily exist in a solar system that is only about 6,000 years old, even without a Kuiper Belt or an Oort cloud.

SECULAR EXPLANATIONS FOR COMETS

Secular scientists believe that comets formed during the formation of the solar system about 4.5 billion years ago. But comets lose their mass so rapidly that none should exist at all today if the solar system really were billions of years old! Secular scientists are well aware of this problem and have proposed two sources to replenish this dwindling comet supply: the Kuiper Belt and the Oort cloud.

KUIPER BELT

The Kuiper Belt is a hypothetical disk of trillions of comet-size icy bodies that secular scientists believe orbit beyond Neptune. They think some of these icy bodies are disrupted from their orbits and redirected into the inner solar system where they become *short-period comets*—comets that require less than 200 years to make a single orbit of the sun. But to replenish the solar system's comets, the Kuiper Belt would need to contain *many* more icy bodies than the mere hundreds that have so far been observed beyond Neptune, and most objects discovered in this area are much larger than typical comet nuclei.

OORT CLOUD

Another supposed source for comets is the Oort cloud, an enormous hypothetical reservoir of comet nuclei thought to surround our solar system. Secular scientists believe the Oort cloud is a source for *long-period comets*—those having orbital periods greater than 200 years. But this alleged cloud is (conveniently) located too far away to be seen, even with our most powerful telescopes. This means there is *zero* observational evidence that it exists!

DID YOU KNOW?

Based on the rate of material lost while orbiting the sun, a typical comet could last no longer than 100,000 years.

CENTAURS

In 1977, astronomer Charles Kowal observed a large asteroid that developed a comet-like tail as it passed close to the sun. This new minor planet seemed like a combination of an asteroid and a comet, so he called it a *centaur*. So far, hundreds of centaurs have been discovered, most of them orbiting between Jupiter and Neptune.

Shedding Light on Black Holes

Black holes are often used to thicken the plot of science fiction novels. They are shrouded in mystery, but scientists know more about them than you might think. Astronomers believe that stellar mass black holes form when extremely large stars burn all of their hydrogen fuel, become unstable, and explode. The explosion blasts a portion of the star's outer layer into space, creating a colorful supernova remnant that is visible in telescopes for centuries. The rest of the star collapses in on itself, while gravity squeezes all of that matter into a very, very tiny amount of space. If the mass of the collapsing star matter is large enough, the entire molecular and atomic structure will collapse under its own weight and get increasingly smaller. This creates a *gravitational well* so strong that light cannot escape—a black hole!

DID YOU KNOW?

Black holes are so dense and their gravity is so strong, even light can't escape if it comes close to them.

TYPES OF BLACK HOLES

If a star with the same mass as our sun collapses, astronomers believe it will become a white dwarf. A white dwarf is a "dead" star that gives off a final glow like an ember in a dying campfire. Although it has a very dense mass, it's not quite large enough to collapse at the atomic level and become a black hole.

But if a star 10 or 20 times the mass of our sun collapses, it will collapse into a *stellar mass black hole*. There may be millions of stellar mass black holes in our galaxy, the Milky Way.

Supermassive black holes are millions or even billions of times more massive than the sun. These lurking giants appear to lie at the center of every large galaxy. They act as gravitational anchors for stars near the core.

We have a supermassive black hole at the center of the Milky Way called *Sagittarius A**. Its mass equals about four million suns and its radius matches about 2,000 Earths. Some scientists think that the biggest supermassive black holes may be up to 20 billion times the mass of our sun.

Some evidence suggests there is a class of *intermediate mass black holes*. These would have a mass between their stellar mass and supermassive cousins.

HOW CAN SCIENTISTS DETECT BLACK HOLES?

Since supermassive black holes lie at the center of galaxies, dust and gas often obscure them. Scientists can see the radiation emitted as the dust and gas are drawn into the supermassive black holes. The edge of the black hole, where matter and light lose their ability to escape, is called the *event horizon.* At this edge, everything enters the black hole—it's the point of no return. Stars can actually orbit black holes, which helps scientists to identify them. Identifying black holes is similar to "seeing" the wind; you don't actually see it, but you see its effects upon nearby objects.

Albert Einstein

Globular star cluster

DID YOU KNOW?

In 1915, Albert Einstein published his general theory of relativity, which physicist Karl Schwarzschild used to predict the existence of black holes. The first one wasn't discovered until 1971. Many of the century-old theories Einstein developed about matter, space, time, and the universe have been proven by modern science.

WILL EARTH SOMEDAY FALL INTO A GIANT BLACK HOLE?

Black holes are not close enough to our solar system to swallow Earth. Even though 100 billion visible galaxies fill the universe, and all of them appear to have black holes, they are too far away to harm us.

Scientists certainly have more to learn and understand about black holes. But even with the knowledge we have, we can appreciate how they show God's creativity, power, and variety in the making of His universe.

Naturalistic Speculations

Naturalistic scientists believe that everything in the universe developed by natural processes and that nothing should be explained by a divine Creator. But when they claim that an explosion created the universe, naturalists present themselves with numerous challenges. The appearance of design must be explained away by chance, they must explain order with chaos, and what looks young has to be explained away as old. Naturalistic theories propose answers to some of the biggest questions of science, but are their ideas based on good interpretations of the evidence? And how do those ideas compare with the Bible?

NATURALISTIC VIEW OF THE UNIVERSE'S COMPOSITION		
AMOUNT	TYPE	SUBSTANCE
5%	Ordinary matter	Protons, Neutrons, and Atoms
27%	Dark matter	Unknown
68%	Dark energy	Unknown

DARK MATTER

Many cosmologists believe that the "ordinary" matter we're familiar with—composed of protons and neutrons that make up atoms—is only a small fraction of all the matter in the universe. The rest is thought to be invisible or "dark" because it doesn't emit the kind of radiation we can detect. This dark matter supposedly makes up nearly 27% of the universe and nearly 80% of its matter.

Scientists inferred the existence of dark matter based on its gravitational effects on spiral galaxies. However, the Big Bang model predicts that the explosion that started the universe would only have produced enough ordinary matter to make up around 20% of the matter thought to exist. Since the Big Bang cannot produce enough protons and neutrons to "fill up" the remaining amount, this matter must be something else. (Other forms of matter exist, but they generally don't have the needed properties for secular models of star and galaxy formation.)

For this reason, Big Bang scientists have to claim that the remaining 80% must be a never-before-observed kind of matter. But even if they find this exotic dark matter, the Big Bang is still in trouble. The current version of the Big Bang can't account for it for the simple reason that no one knows what dark matter is! Dark matter may or may not exist, but it requires faith for secular cosmologists to believe that something that cannot be seen, touched, or detected is the explanation for what they observe.

DARK ENERGY

Some clues suggest the universe is expanding. You might think gravity would slow down the expansion, but secular scientists have concluded that it is actually speeding up. This would require some kind of "antigravity" energy that secular scientists call *dark energy*.

Dark energy speculation helps show the weakness of the Big Bang model. When you add up all the forms of energy that are thought to exist (radiation, dark energy, the energy in matter, etc.), it turns out that ordinary matter would only make up 5% of all the "stuff" in the universe. The other 95% would be exotic dark matter and dark energy. This means Big Bang advocates are claiming that they can explain how the universe came into being without a Creator while admitting they don't know what 95% of the universe actually is!

Oort Cloud

Every time a comet gets close to the sun and develops a tail, it loses some of its material. For this reason, comets can only last at most 100,000 years or so. Since naturalistic scientists believe the solar system and its comets are billions of years old, they must propose some way to produce new comets.

Supposedly, the chunks of icy debris that make up a hypothetical Oort cloud are sometimes dislodged and fall inward toward the solar system. These particles become comets, and as older comets disintegrate, new ones form to take their place.

Unfortunately for secular scientists, no evidence supports such a cloud. It merely sidesteps the simple fact that comets should not still exist if our solar system were really billions of years old.

Multiverse

The Big Bang had some pretty big problems when it was first proposed, so the inflation theory was added to try to solve them (see pages 22-23). Theorists now speculate that inflation would result in a multiverse with an infinite number of universes. Some secular scientists think we are simply "lucky" enough to live in a universe whose laws of physics and chemistry allow life to exist.

However, there is no evidence for other universes. And their possible existence wouldn't explain why life exists here since the laws of physics in our universe actually prevent life coming from non-life. Therefore, secular scientists gain nothing by making this argument, and a supernatural Creator is still required to explain our existence.

"Naturalism is based on a tiny subset of truth whereas creationism is based on the absolute, though not exhaustive, truth of the biblical account. After all, man was not present until the sixth day of creation, but God was present as an eyewitness at the very beginning. All men believe something, the only difference is where or in whom they place that faith."[4]

—Vernon R. Cupps, Ph.D.
Nuclear Physicist

Evidence for a Young Universe

Secular scientists believe the universe resulted from a cosmic accident billions of years ago, but this origins account contradicts Genesis. Using genealogies and historical events mentioned in Scripture to calculate the biblical timescale, we find that our universe should only be about 6,000 years old—not billions. Interestingly, creation scientists are finding significant evidence that points to a recent creation by an intentional and masterful Designer. Check out these fascinating features of our universe that harmonize with the Genesis account.

SATURN'S RINGS

Many planets have rings, but we see Saturn's so easily because they're wide and bright. The rings are made of 90% water-ice and should darken with age. Secular scientists acknowledge that it's difficult to reconcile their "new and shiny" appearance with billions of years.

IO'S VOLCANOES

Jupiter's moon Io has more volcanic activity than anything else in our solar system. Its volcanoes give off over 90,000 gigawatts of heat! Secular scientists think it might go through cycles of geological activity, aided by the gravitational pulls of other moons. But after millions of years, Io should be cold and dark. Its excessive heat fits a young universe— one that has been cooling for only about 6,000 years.

Io's volcano Pele

VENUS' VOLCANOES

Astronomers from Brown University were shocked to discover evidence of active volcanoes on Venus. Like Io, volcanic activity is a strong sign of youth—if Venus is billions of years old that kind of internal energy should have been used up long ago.

Volcanoes on Venus

ENCELADUS' GEYSERS

As Enceladus swings around Saturn, this moon leaves a trail of water vapor and ice particles thanks to 101 powerful geysers erupting from its southern hemisphere. It isn't even the width of Arizona and yet its geysers give off over 16 gigawatts of heat and 375 kilograms of water per second. When pent-up energy spews this quickly, it doesn't take long to run out. Secular scientists think Enceladus could have started out with enough energy for the geysers to last 10 million years, but that's far younger than its secular age estimate. Enceladus gives all the signs of being young.

Geyser on Enceladus

Titan

PLANETARY MAGNETIC FIELDS

Many planets have a magnetic field. Earth's protects us from harmful solar radiation—a vital feature for life to survive. Scientists have measured the rate of its decay over the last 200 years or so. Calculating backward, we find that magnetic fields decay too quickly to be millions or billions of years old. If Earth's magnetic field were more than 50,000 years old, it would be gone. Magnetic fields are like clocks that give us a maximum age of a planet—and they tell us that many planets in our solar system can't be very old.

MERCURY'S DECAYING FIELD RATE

In 1984, creation physicist Russell Humphreys used measurements from *Mariner 10*'s 1975 Mercury visit to predict how fast the planet's magnetic field would decay from an assumed full strength of 6,000 years ago. The data *Messenger* collected in 2008 closely matched his predicted lower field strength, showing that the field is decaying too fast to be eons old. Mercury's magnetic field could be thousands of years old—but certainly not millions.

COMETS

Comets are big masses of ice and dirt that orbit the sun. They're like dirty snowballs. Secular scientists place their ages at around 4.5 billion years old. However, comets lose mass every time they encounter the sun's heat. They should all have disintegrated after only a few thousand years. How could they be billions of years old?

PLUTO'S SURFACE

In 2015 after a nine-year voyage, the *New Horizons* spacecraft whizzed by Pluto, taking pictures as it passed. The mission gave us unprecedented insight into the dwarf planet. Images of Pluto's smooth plains reveal a young surface that shows no signs of eons of cosmic bombardments.

TITAN'S ATMOSPHERE

Saturn's biggest moon, Titan, has a thick atmosphere of nitrogen with traces of methane. Sunlight destroys methane. According to secular researchers, Titan's methane atmosphere should only survive a few tens of millions of years of sunshine, though they believe Titan itself has existed for billions. Titan's methane is a significant sign of youth.

Comet Lovejoy

BLUE STARS

Blue stars are some of the biggest and brightest stars in the universe. They contain much more hydrogen than other stars but also burn out much more quickly. Blue stars can't last longer than a few million years, yet we find them all over the universe. Secular scientists explain their presence by claiming that new stars are being born to replace the dying ones. To date, no one has observed a star being formed or discovered the millions of supernova remnants we would expect to see after billions of years of dying stars.

Pluto

"You are worthy, O Lord, to receive glory and honor and power; for You created all things, and by Your will they exist and were created." (Revelation 4:11)

A Tribute to the Hubble Space Telescope

Named after the famous astronomer Edwin Hubble, the Hubble Space Telescope is the largest and most recognizable space instrument for the observation and photography of the universe. It allows us to peer deeper into the heavens than we ever have before—and its images are breathtaking. The farther we look, the more of God's creativity and awesome handiwork we see written across the cosmos.

EDWIN HUBBLE

People remember Edwin Hubble best for the telescope that carries his name. While serving on staff at the Mount Wilson Observatory in California, Hubble confirmed that distant "island universes" were actually galaxies like our own and classified them. He also famously discovered the relationship between redshift and distance, which led to the theory that the universe is expanding.

The Hubble Telescope

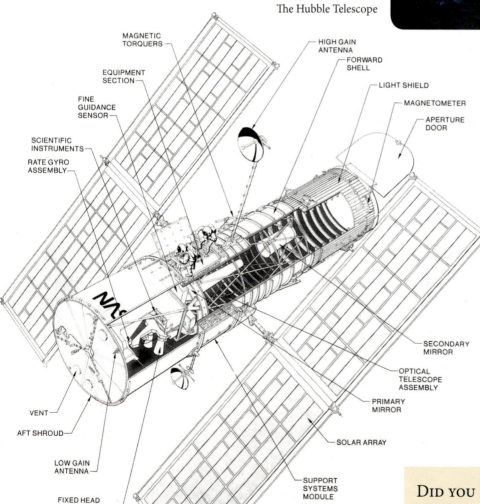

MAGNETIC TORQUERS

HIGH GAIN ANTENNA

FORWARD SHELL

EQUIPMENT SECTION

LIGHT SHIELD

FINE GUIDANCE SENSOR

MAGNETOMETER

APERTURE DOOR

SCIENTIFIC INSTRUMENTS

RATE GYRO ASSEMBLY

SECONDARY MIRROR

OPTICAL TELESCOPE ASSEMBLY

PRIMARY MIRROR

VENT

AFT SHROUD

SOLAR ARRAY

LOW GAIN ANTENNA

SUPPORT SYSTEMS MODULE

FIXED HEAD STAR TRACKERS

FINDING FUNDS

After World War II, NASA wanted to use some of the new rocket technology scientists developed during the war for space exploration. They planned to build the Hubble Space Telescope as a satellite so it could take deep-space pictures. Since government funds were scarce and NASA didn't have the resources to take on this project, astronomers led a nationwide effort to raise funds. They met with congressmen and women and launched large-scale letter-writing campaigns, and eventually the government gave them half of the funds they needed. Though NASA reduced the planned size for the Hubble Space Telescope to fit their lesser budget, they had enough to begin.

Edwin Hubble

DID YOU KNOW?

The Hubble's mirror needed to be polished to an accuracy of 10 nanometers so it could capture and reflect light with incredible precision.

CONSTRUCTION

Once they had enough money to build the Hubble, NASA divided responsibilities among several organizations. One organization innovated the telescope's design, development, and construction, while a second controlled its instruments and overall mission command. A third focused solely on building the mirrors and sensors. And a fourth organization built a spacecraft to house the telescope. After 12 years of construction, the Hubble Space Telescope launched in 1990.

Carina Nebula

Spiral galaxy

DID YOU KNOW?

The Hubble Space Telescope can lock on to distant cosmic targets without deviating even the width of a human hair!

UPGRADES AND MAINTENANCE

Not long after the Hubble's launch, NASA discovered that the primary mirror had an incorrect curvature. They installed optical corrections three years later. Over the course of its mission, NASA has serviced the telescope five times—updating old instruments, installing new ones, upgrading computer software, replacing gyroscopes, and so on.

A MAGNIFICENT MISSION

Scientists control the telescope from the ground, and solar panels keep it powered. Among its greatest accomplishments, the Hubble has taken deep-space images, imaged extrasolar planets, and analyzed spectra to determine the distance of cosmic objects. Even after the Hubble Space Telescope retires, we can continue to benefit from the legacy of the astounding images it will leave behind.

Eagle Nebula

The Space Shuttle Program

We often marvel at spaceships in the movies, but real space travel isn't always so glamorous. Instead of hopping into a slick space-jet, astronauts climb aboard a craft that has taken a lot of time, money, and talent to put together. And the launch itself can be risky. Nowadays, rockets blast U.S. astronauts into space solely from Russian space facilities, but NASA's Space Shuttle program used to conduct its own launches.

WHAT WAS THE SPACE SHUTTLE PROGRAM?

In 1972, the same year the Apollo missions to the moon ended, President Richard Nixon funded NASA's Space Shuttle program. It built iconic space shuttles that were used to put satellites into orbit, place and maintain the Hubble Space Telescope, and convey astronauts to the International Space Station. The first space shuttle launched in 1981, and the program was retired in 2011. The entire 30-year venture cost around $209 billion.

DID YOU KNOW?

NASA's shuttles clocked in around 198,728.5 man-hours in space. That's about 8,280 days!

THE SHUTTLES' JOB

NASA space shuttles were partially reusable spacecraft that could carry people and equipment into space and orbit around Earth, but they were not designed to travel as far as the moon. Space shuttles were used to repair satellites and deliver equipment and crew to the International Space Station. A back hatch on the shuttles could open to deploy large satellites like the Hubble Space Telescope and could transport large payloads.

NASA built five shuttles: *Columbia, Challenger, Discovery, Atlantis,* and *Endeavor*. Altogether they performed 135 launches. However, two of them (*Challenger* and *Columbia*) suffered catastrophic accidents during their final missions, killing their crews.

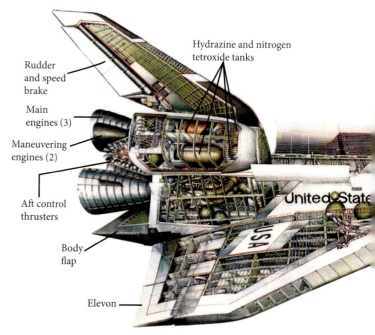

Hydrazine and nitrogen tetroxide tanks

Rudder and speed brake

Main engines (3)

Maneuvering engines (2)

Aft control thrusters

Body flap

Elevon

United States

USA

DID YOU KNOW?

Each space shuttle launch cost around $450 million.

FIRST LIFTOFF

Columbia (1981)

Challenger (1983)

Discovery (1984)

Atlantis (1985)

Endeavour (1992)

COLUMBIA   CHALLENGER   DISCOVERY   ATLANTIS   ENDEAVOUR

COOPERATING SPACE CENTERS

Several American space centers participated in the Space Shuttle program, including the Kennedy Space Center in Florida, Vandenberg Air Force Base in California, the Johnson Space Center in Houston, Marshall Space Flight Center in Alabama, John C. Stennis Space Center in Mississippi, and the Goddard Space Flight Center in Maryland.

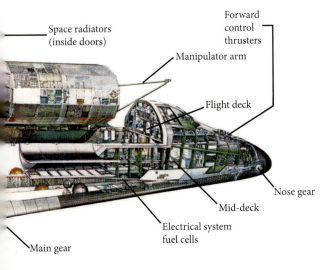

Space radiators (inside doors)
Forward control thrusters
Manipulator arm
Flight deck
Nose gear
Mid-deck
Electrical system fuel cells
Main gear

SHUTTLE CONSTRUCTION

Space shuttles consisted of three parts: an orbiter vehicle (the white ship), an expendable external tank that contained liquid hydrogen and liquid oxygen (the large bullet-shaped object), and a pair of recoverable solid rocket boosters (slender crayon-shaped objects on either side of the external tank). Altogether, each shuttle stood around 184.2 feet long and had a diameter of around 28.5 feet.

DID YOU KNOW?

In NASA's program, the orbiter usually carried five to seven crew members, and they launched from the Kennedy Space Center in Florida.

The *Atlantis* crew May 2009

The first *Discovery* launch (1984)

LAUNCH

Space shuttles performed a two-stage ascent. Two minutes after liftoff, the two white rocket boosters released and parachuted into the ocean, and ships retrieved them for reuse. Meanwhile, the orbiter and the external tank continued on an increasingly horizontal path until they reached orbital speed. At this point, the external tank disconnected and burned up in the atmosphere. The orbiter then conducted its mission.

Fascinating Space Facts

Relax and read on for a few intriguing space facts! Some will amuse, some will surprise, and others will make your jaw drop. But either way, we can't help but marvel at the unfathomable wonders of God's creation.

Halley's Comet passes the earth every 75-76 years. We won't see it again until 2061.

There is no sound in space! Air is needed to transmit sound, and space doesn't have any.

A light-year is about 5.88 trillion miles.

Astronauts can't burp in space!

Astronauts' first footprints on the moon could last a very long time since there's no wind to blow them away.

Earth is the only planet in the solar system not named after a Greek or Roman god.

About one million Earths could fit inside the sun.

Venus spins backward compared to other planets in our solar system.

Because of thick gases in its atmosphere that create a greenhouse effect, Venus is the hottest planet in our solar system.

A day on Venus lasts longer than its year.

The moon moves away from the earth about 1.6 inches each year.

The International Astronomical Union classified Pluto as a dwarf planet in 2006.

Mercury and Venus don't have any moons.

All of the planets in our solar system could fit inside Jupiter.

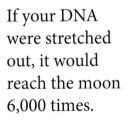

Uranus' unique tilt and long orbit cause a night near its poles to last 21 years.

The moon takes 27.32 days to orbit Earth.

When liquid floats in space, it forms a sphere.

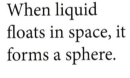

If your DNA were stretched out, it would reach the moon 6,000 times.

One planet bigger than Earth might be made of diamonds! It's 4,000 light-years away.

Man on the Moon

"That's one small step for [a] man, one giant leap for mankind," Neil Armstrong declared after his space boots hit the surface of the moon in 1969. This journey began just after World War II, when the United States and the Soviet Union emerged as dominant world powers. The two countries competed to see who could develop the most advanced space technology and prove to be the superior world power. After only a decade of sending rockets and probes beyond Earth's atmosphere, America put a man on the moon. This moment signified one of the greatest scientific and technological achievements of mankind.

APOLLO 11

Apollo 11 was the first manned mission to the moon. It had three crewmembers: Neil Armstrong, Buzz Aldrin, and Michael Collins. The mission launched on July 16, 1969, and landed on the moon in the Sea of Tranquility on July 20. On July 21, Neil Armstrong was the first man to step on the moon. Buzz Aldrin followed a few minutes later. They walked for about 2.5 hours and collected about 47.5 pounds of lunar material. The third crew member, Michael Collins, piloted the Command Module that remained in the moon's orbit waiting for the return of the Lunar Module. Apollo 11 returned to Earth on July 24, splashing down in the Pacific Ocean. The mission lasted about eight days.

Neil Armstrong took this picture of Buzz Aldrin on the surface of the moon.

APOLLO 11 SPACECRAFT

Three modules composed the Apollo 11 spacecraft: the Command Module with a cabin for three astronauts; a Service Module that propelled the Command Module and provided electrical power, oxygen, and water; and a Lunar Module used for landing on the moon. NASA named the Lunar Module *Eagle* after America's national bird. The Command Module was named *Columbia* after the *Columbiad*, a fictional spacecraft fired from a giant cannon to the moon in Jules Verne's 1865 novel *From the Earth to the Moon*.

Buzz Aldrin's bootprint on the moon

FUN FACTS

- Moments after stepping on the moon, Buzz Aldrin called it a "magnificent desolation."
- Neil Armstrong walked a maximum of 196 feet from the *Eagle* Lunar Module.
- The astronauts left a few commemorative objects on the moon's surface: medallions bearing the names of the three Apollo 1 astronauts who lost their lives in a launch pad fire and two cosmonauts who also died in accidents, as well as a one-and-a-half-inch silicon disk containing micro-miniaturized goodwill messages from 73 countries and the names of congressional and NASA leaders.
- The three astronauts of Apollo 11 were quarantined for 21 days upon returning from the moon. This was a safety measure against unknown diseases or bacteria.

Apollo 17 mission commander Eugene A. Cernan drives the Lunar Roving Vehicle.

OTHER MISSIONS TO THE MOON

Six manned missions have made it to the moon's surface. They happened over a 41-month period from July 1969 to December 1972. A total of 12 men have walked on the moon.

Missions	Landed on the Moon
Apollo 11	July 20, 1969
Apollo 12	November 19, 1969
Apollo 14	February 5, 1971
Apollo 15	July 30, 1971
Apollo 16	April 21, 1972
Apollo 17	December 11, 1972

DID YOU KNOW?

The Soviets were the first to put an unmanned probe on the moon. It was the *Luna 2* mission, which impacted on the surface September 14, 1959.

Harrison H. Schmitt, Apollo 17

APOLLO 13

Apollo 13 was scheduled to land on the moon, but during the journey one of the oxygen tanks exploded, causing severe damage to the Service Module. The crew had to completely shut down the Command Module to save its energy for re-entry into Earth's atmosphere and used the Lunar Module as a kind of lifeboat. After remarkable efforts by the astronauts and Mission Control, the crew made it safely back to Earth on April 17, 1970. Several film adaptations have been made of the dramatic events of Apollo 13.

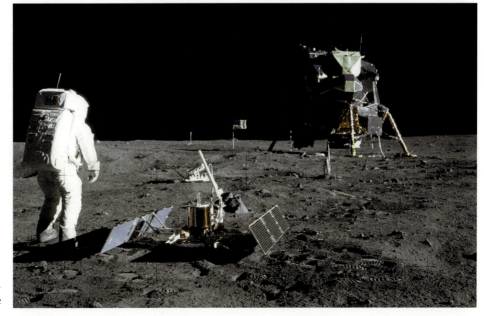

Buzz Aldrin with the Passive Seismic Experiment Package and *Eagle* Lunar Module

How to Be an Astronaut

Did you ever wish you were an astronaut sailing among the stars? Well, it's possible! NASA receives many applications from all kinds of people. The competition is stiff and the road is long, but if you think you might be a good fit, you should get started right away!

DID YOU KNOW?

The name "astronaut" is derived from the Greek words *astron* (star) and *nautes* (sailor). An astronaut is a star sailor!

EDUCATION

As a first step, study a STEM discipline. This means getting a four-year degree in either science, technology, engineering, or mathematics. Astronauts use these skills constantly, so it's essential that you immerse yourself in them.

EXPERIENCE

You should also get a pilot's license and clock in some flying time. You need at least 1,000 hours of pilot experience or three years of related experience.

ADDITIONAL EXPERIENCE

NASA is looking for well-rounded individuals. Know science, get a pilot's license, and learn to play guitar! Or the violin, it doesn't matter which. What matters is demonstrating capability and excellence in many things—like learning musical instruments, playing sports, or going on outside-the-box adventures. This shows that you think creatively and can adapt to many different scenarios.

BODY TYPE

Not anyone can apply to be an astronaut. In height, you need to stand between 62 and 75 inches. Spaceship quarters are tight, and you need to be short enough to fit but also tall enough to reach the controls. You also need to be slim and in great shape—which means a lot of exercise.

APPLY

After years of preparation, you're ready to apply to be an astronaut. NASA accepts applications every three to five years with four minimum requirements:

1. Be a United States citizen.
2. Have a bachelor's degree in a STEM discipline.
3. Have adequate related field experience.
4. Meet certain weight and height restrictions.

ELIMINATION PROCESS

Many, many people apply. For only a dozen open astronaut positions in 2016, NASA received over 18,000 applications! However, most of them don't meet the basic requirements and that shortens the list of potential candidates to only a few thousand. NASA reviews the remainders by looking at the "whole package" (this is where being a well-rounded individual helps) and narrows the field down to a few hundred. Then they check references. Only a few dozen remain. Most astronauts have to apply multiple times before they are chosen.

INTERVIEW

NASA interviews the remaining applicants, and each interview lasts about an hour. By this point, they already know that you're qualified, so they are checking to see if you're the kind of person who can work well with others and would be a good fit for the team. It's all about a positive impression. In addition to the interview, you'll have to go through physical and psychological exams. If you go to the International Space Station, you have to be in excellent physical and psychological condition.

NASA astronaut Scott Kelly in training

TRAIN

If you pass the interview process, then you're an astronaut! Congratulations! You are among only a few chosen out of thousands of applicants. But it's not over yet. You will have to go through two years of training. You will become a qualified scuba diver, do military water survival training, pass swimming tests, become exposed to a variety of atmospheric pressures, learn Russian, and gain many other skills. You will travel the world while training. It'll be tough, but that's okay…you're an *astronaut*.

LAUNCH

After years of training, you're ready to… wait. You don't get to launch immediately. Only three American astronauts are chosen per year to ride on the Soyuz rocket with the Russians to the International Space Station, and many astronauts must wait several years before they actually get to launch into space. The missions last between six months and a year. But eventually you'll get to shoot to the stars.

Cosmonaut Alexey Ovchinin, NASA astronaut Jeff Williams, and cosmonaut Oleg Skripochka of Expedition 47 wave goodbye just before heading to the Soyuz spacecraft that rocketed them to the International Space Station on March 18, 2016.

The Human Body in Space

God created Earth with the ideal conditions for humans to thrive. So when astronauts leave Earth's well-suited environment and enter space, it's a whole new ballgame. Space, stunning as it is, presents a hostile environment for people—and all other living creatures. The microgravity, exposure to high levels of solar radiation, lack of oxygen, and other factors make space dangerous for astronauts unless they have the proper protection. Though scientists are working on better accommodations, space still has unusual effects on the human body.

NASA astronaut Scott Kelly after his return to Earth on March 1, 2016

HEIGHT

On Earth, gravity pulls down on the spine, compressing each vertebra. But in space an astronaut's spine elongates, and he or she temporarily grows an inch or so taller.

HEART

In space, the heart doesn't pump as strongly because it's not having to circulate blood against gravity. With less exertion the heart gets smaller.

BALANCE

Astronauts' sensorimotor functions depend upon the presence of gravity. Without it, they have to use visual cues to stay upright. They can't stay balanced if they close their eyes, and it takes several hours for their sense of balance to adjust after returning to Earth.

BONES AND MUSCLES

Earth's gravity provides the resistance needed to develop strong muscles and bones. During extended periods in space, astronauts must mimic this resistance by using specialized exercise equipment. Though exercise helps temper the effects, an astronaut's muscles and bones still atrophy over time.

EYES

Since the air pressure in space differs from Earth, astronauts' eyeballs change shape. They keep many different prescriptions of glasses on space missions so they can compensate for their vision changes.

Left: Using the Advanced Diagnostic Ultrasound in Microgravity (ADUM) protocols, ISS Expedition Commander Leroy Chiao performs an ultrasound examination of the eye on Flight Engineer Salizhan Sharipov.

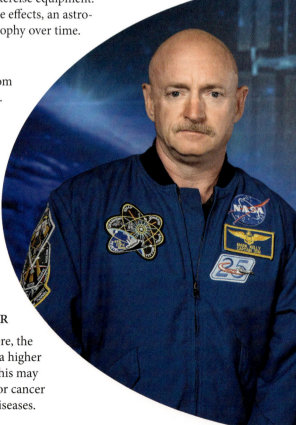

SPEECH

Astronauts' lips and tongues work differently without gravity, so their speech changes in space. Canadian astronaut Chris Hadfield described the sensation upon returning to Earth during a 2013 press conference: "Right after I landed, I could feel the weight of my lips and tongue and I had to change how I was talking. I hadn't realized that I learned to talk with a weightless tongue."[5]

RADIATION DANGER

Beyond Earth's atmosphere, the human body encounters a higher level of solar radiation. This may result in long-term risk for cancer and other degenerative diseases.

WITHOUT PROTECTION

The specially crafted features of a spacesuit, spacecraft, and space station provide vital protection for an astronaut in space. Without them:

- The sun's ultraviolet rays burn any exposed skin.
- The body swells to twice its normal size.
- Air in the lungs expands and explodes.
- Fluids in the eyes, mouth, and nose freeze.
- Oxygen in the blood dissolves through the skin.
- Blood vessels enlarge and the heart can no longer pump blood fast enough to live.
- Blood boils due to low pressure.

With these terrible effects, a person can't survive for more than a few seconds unprotected in space. Training, research, and technology help ensure an astronaut's safety.

EXTRAVEHICULAR MOBILITY UNIT

The Extravehicular Mobility Unit (EMU) spacesuit was first used in the Space Shuttle program in 1982 and is still in use today on the International Space Station. It weighs around 254 pounds, with a life support backpack. The EMU protects astronauts from the hazards of space when they do spacewalks. Its primary life support lasts around eight hours, and a backup life support offers an extra 30 minutes. Fitted with 14 different layers, each suit costs around $12 million to produce.

EMU spacesuit

Z-2 spacesuit

Z-2 SPACESUIT

After three decades of using the EMU, NASA is putting the final touches on a new spacesuit called the Z-2. Designed with Mars exploration in mind, its higher air pressure will eliminate the need to breathe oxygen for two hours before a spacewalk. The suit will also connect to the outside of any spacecraft and allow an astronaut to simply climb in, seal off, and disconnect. This suit will be cheaper, more efficient, more mobile, and actually look a little stylish.

Astronauts
Mark Kelly (left) and
Scott Kelly (right)

THE TWINS STUDY

Astronauts Scott and Mark Kelly were the first siblings to fly in space, and they happen to be identical twins. NASA's Human Research Program is conducting the Twins Study to observe physical differences between the men after Scott completed a year aboard the International Space Station and Mark spent a year on Earth. Researchers expect to discover some of the more subtle effects and changes that may occur in spaceflight because they will be comparing two men with the same genetic makeup.

Science Fiction vs. Reality

Many people enjoy a good science fiction movie. Spaceships traveling at light speed, epic space dogfights, teleportation, laser blasters—all super cool stuff. But is any of it actually possible? Some of these inventions will likely remain only on the silver screen. However, scientists have had some success bringing others to reality. Only God knows what will happen in the future, but we can speculate about the technological possibilities.

TELEPORTATION

The idea that matter can be moved between locations without actually traveling the distance was popularized in the original 1960s *Star Trek* series. The concept might seem impossible, but scientists have actually had some small experimental success, like teleporting an atom from one room to another. *Quantum entanglement*, a phenomenon of quantum physics, allows particles to be connected to each other regardless of distance. It doesn't matter if two particles are 10 feet away or 10 light-years away—they will still be connected on a subatomic level. Changing one will instantly change the other. Some physicists say this phenomenon allows for human teleportation in the distant future.

HOLOGRAPHY

Holography, as presented in many science fiction franchises, is possible. Scientists have successfully built rudimentary 3-D holograms and even tiny touchable ones visible in daylight. Advanced holography might become commercialized within the next few decades.

WORMHOLES

Many speculate on wormholes in the universe that connect to each other by bending space and time. Travel between them would be instantaneous—perhaps crossing billions of light-years. No observable evidence supports wormholes, but theories of general relativity allow them to be possible. It would be like having a 2-D plane with a circular tunnel that leads out of one place and appears elsewhere on the plane. Except in a 3-D environment, like our universe, the wormholes would appear spherical.

TRAVELING AT LIGHT SPEED

Light speed looks great in movies. Unfortunately, it's impossible. Traveling at light speed would require an infinite energy source, which simply does not exist in our universe. Anyway, even traveling at light speed, it would still take thousands of years to travel between galaxies, as measured by clocks on Earth.

HYPERDRIVE

"Punch the hyperdrive!" Though traveling at light speed is impossible, traveling at *very high* speeds can be accomplished…with some technological advancement. With sufficient energy, it is possible—in principle—to travel at *almost* the speed of light. But such energies are far beyond our current technology.

LIGHTSABERS

Lightsabers are iconic weapons, flashing green and red as Luke Skywalker fights Darth Vader in *Return of the Jedi*. Yet as cool as they look onscreen, lightsabers simply are not possible in the foreseeable technological future. They are supposedly made of lasers, but lasers can't just extend one meter and then stop. They need something to block them. Also, lasers don't make humming noises, cannot be seen from the side, and pass through objects instead of clashing against them.

RAY GUNS

"Set to stun." Ray guns and their like abound in science fiction. They have varying abilities and functions, but they're usually lethal, have distinct heated pulses, and perform like modern guns. However, lasers, light, plasma, and other fictional gun elements can't function the way they do in the movies. They can't be slowed down below the speed of light, they're often invisible, and don't make noises. Basically, they're improbable for the same reasons lightsabers are improbable.

ARTIFICIAL INTELLIGENCE

As far back as ancient Greece, humans have speculated on intelligent machines. The concept made its way into many modern science fiction films, like *2001: A Space Odyssey.* Computer scientists have built machines that can mimic human thinking—such as a search engine that predicts what you're searching for—but so far actual intelligence hasn't been achieved. Some scientists speculate on the possibility of artificial intelligence, but it will likely never happen. Machines cannot have God-given traits like a soul, mind, conscience, or emotions. These spiritual aspects cannot be broken down into particles and computer code.

Building the International Space Station

The Space Race of the 1950s generated a lot of excitement and innovative technology—and culminated in 1969 with man's first step on the moon! But today Russia, America, and many other nations around the world no longer compete in space. They now work together to advance space exploration, and one major accomplishment of this collaboration is the International Space Station (ISS).

WHAT IS THE ISS?

The ISS is an orbiting laboratory. It normally houses six crew members who perform experiments in a range of scientific fields. These experiments are solicited by nations all around the world who helped build and now help manage the ISS. The station also acts as a staging base for possible future missions to the moon, Mars, and asteroids.

HOW IT WAS BUILT

Construction of the ISS began in 1998 with the launch of the Russian module Zarya. Two weeks later, the United States launched Unity, which was then attached to Zarya. In 2000, the Russians launched Zvezda, which added living quarters. The first resident crew of three astronauts arrived in November 2000. Since then, the ISS has had a continual human presence, and many more modules and parts have been added to it. The project has cost over $120 billion to build.

DID YOU KNOW?

The ISS orbits Earth every 90 minutes. That's about 16 times per day.

IN ORBIT

The ISS orbits about 250 miles above the Earth. It travels about 17,500 miles per hour—that's around five miles per second! At that speed, it could travel to the moon and back in a day.

DID YOU KNOW?

In May 2012, the SpaceX *Dragon* was the first private (nongovernment) spacecraft to visit the ISS.

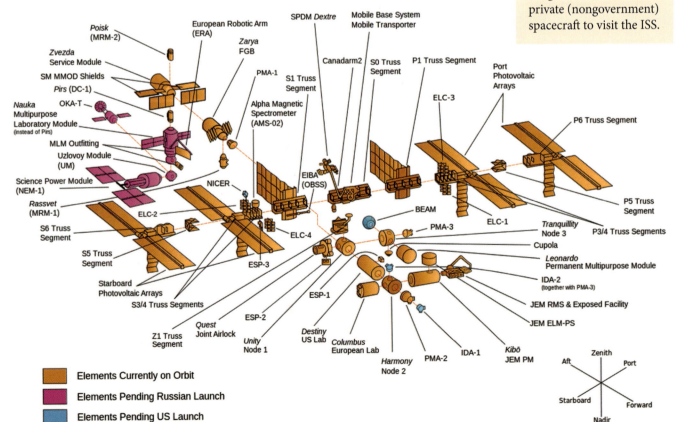

Elements Currently on Orbit

Elements Pending Russian Launch

Elements Pending US Launch

MODULES

The ISS has 15 pressurized modules. This means an unsuited astronaut can enter them safely. The pressurized and unpressurized modules are divided into two sections: the Russian Orbital Segment (ROS) and the United States Orbital Segment (USOS). Various nations have contributed modules to the ISS.

WE'RE ALL IN THIS TOGETHER

Sixteen countries helped construct the ISS: the United States, Russia, Canada, Japan, Belgium, Brazil, Denmark, France, Germany, Italy, the Netherlands, Norway, Spain, Sweden, Switzerland, and the United Kingdom.

CONTROL CENTERS

The Roscosmos Mission Control Center in Russia navigates the entire ISS, but other countries control individual parts. Mission Control Centers are working in nations such as Russia, France, Japan, United States, Germany, Canada, India, and China.

LIFE SUPPORT

The atmosphere on the ISS resembles Earth's. The station produces oxygen through a process called *electrolysis*. This uses electricity from solar panels to split water molecules into hydrogen and oxygen gas.

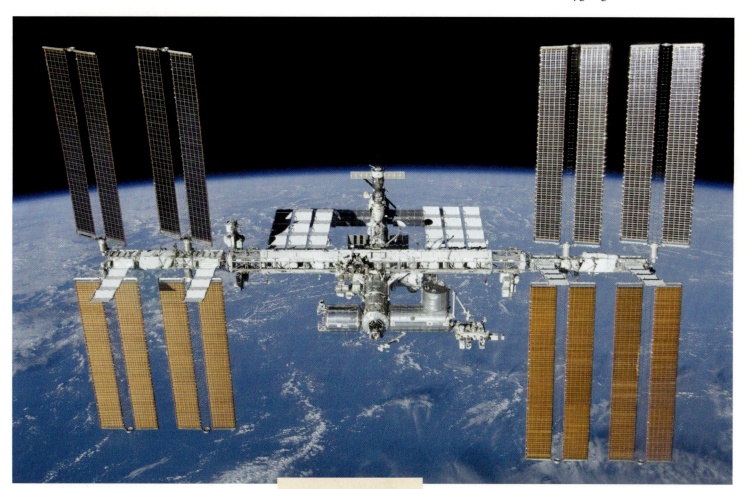

MICROGRAVITY

The effect of Earth's gravity is only slightly weaker aboard the ISS, but the station's orbital speed (17,500 mph) puts objects in a continuous state of freefall that simulates weightlessness. Microgravity helps experiments since fluids can be almost completely combined.

DID YOU KNOW?

The ISS has over eight miles of wiring in its electrical system!

ADDITIONAL FEATURES

Since living in space for an extended time challenges the human body, the ISS was built with reasonable accommodations for its crew. It has two bathrooms, a gymnasium, and even a small, dome-like window so the astronauts can have a good view of Earth. Six robotic arms on the station's exterior assist in experiments, maintenance, and adding new modules.

Life on the International Space Station

After years of work and training, chosen astronauts finally get to launch into space, usually to serve as crew members aboard the International Space Station (ISS). They don't get to take much with them—all of their personal belongings must fit in a very small space. At the ISS, astronauts get to see something very few people ever do: the earth from orbit. While being an astronaut sounds fun, it also involves a lot of work! Most missions last around six months. Here's a glimpse of life on the ISS.

DID YOU KNOW?

ISS crewmembers can drink coffee! Samantha Cristoforetti was the first person to enjoy an espresso in space. This was thanks to a new device called ISSpresso that could brew a cup of coffee in microgravity.

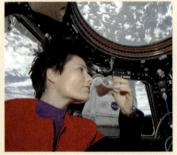

WORK

During most of their workdays, astronauts perform experiments on behalf of nations around the world. Microgravity offers a unique environment for experimentation, such as allowing liquids to combine more fully than on Earth. Astronauts also spend a lot of time maintaining the station. This involves spacewalking to fix the exterior, cleaning air filters, updating computer software, etc. Mission Control closely monitors the station and instructs crew members on what maintenance is needed.

HYGIENE

Astronauts have to get ready in the morning just like you. They brush their teeth, shave, and take a shower. Toothpaste and shaving cream are much the same as on Earth. However, astronauts can't take showers in the same way. Water floats and doesn't rinse. So astronauts use "rinseless" shampoo originally invented for hospital patients who are unable to shower. They also use wet wipes instead of body wash. To go to the bathroom, they use a special toilet that draws in like a vacuum cleaner.

NASA astronaut Kjell Lindgren corrals the supply of fresh fruit that arrived August 25, 2015, on the Kounotori 5 H-II Transfer Vehicle (HTV-5).

EATING

Space food gets a bad rap, but actually it's quite tasty! Some foods, like fruit, can be eaten normally. But others need added water. Salt and pepper are packaged as liquids; otherwise, the tiny grains would float, clogging vents and getting into astronauts' noses and eyes. The ISS also has a refrigerator and oven. According to NASA, astronauts eat things like fruit, nuts, peanut butter, chicken, beef, seafood, candy, and brownies. For drinks, they get tea, orange juice, fruit punches, and lemonade. Nutritionists also make sure that each astronaut gets enough nutrients and calories to help him or her stay healthy throughout the mission.

FREE TIME

It's important to relax after working hard, so astronauts on the ISS get free time every day. They watch movies, read, play cards, communicate with friends and relatives through phone and email, and enjoy many other leisure activities similar to those on Earth. But one special activity that often draws them is looking out the window at the incredible view. Astronaut Jeff Williams says, "The biggest attraction isn't deep space—it's the earth….You never get tired of viewing the earth."[6] He has taken over 330,000 pictures of Earth from orbit!

EXERCISE

Astronauts don't use many muscles while floating around in microgravity. This means they have to exercise two hours a day to prevent bone and muscle loss. Their gymnasium has a treadmill, exercise bike, and other specially designed equipment.

Expedition 21 flight engineer Nicole Stott exercises on the Combined Operational Load Bearing External Resistance Treadmill (COLBERT). A bungee harness keeps her from floating away from the machine.

A TYPICAL DAY

Crews have a schedule to keep. They usually wake up around 6:00 a.m. Coordinated Universal Time. They get ready for the day, inspect the station, eat breakfast, plan their day with Mission Control, then begin their work at around 8:00 a.m. with a two-hour exercise workout. Then the astronauts work eight hours, with a one-hour lunch break. They perform experiments, make repairs to the station, and complete many other important tasks. Including their daily exercise, crewmembers work 10 hours each weekday, five hours on Saturday, and have Sundays off.

DID YOU KNOW?

Luke Skywalker's lightsaber prop from *Return of the Jedi* has been to the ISS!

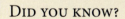

Sleeping cabin on the ISS

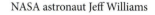

NASA astronaut Jeff Williams

SLEEPING

Each astronaut gets a closet-like cabin with room for one person. A laptop and sleeping bag are attached to the wall. Astronauts are scheduled to sleep eight hours after each workday, and the windows are shut to simulate nighttime. The atmosphere has to be well ventilated or crew members could wake up gasping for air with a bubble of their own carbon dioxide around their heads.

Astronaut Col. Jeffrey N. Williams holds the world record for taking the most photographs in space. He's captured more than 330,000 images from the International Space Station.

Crop circles in West Texas (above); rapeseed and lavender fields near Szombathely, Hungary (below); Deadvlei, Namibia (right)

Sossusvlei dunes in Namib-Naukluft National Park of Namibia

Orange River, South Africa

North Key Largo, Florida

Viedma Glacier, near the border between Chile and Argentina (left); *Dragon* spacecraft (below)

Caution: Astronauts at Work

Astronauts have plenty to do on the International Space Station (ISS). The unique microgravity environment provides a great location for them to conduct scientific experiments. Many of these studies help researchers better understand the effects of space on humans, animals, and objects. Astronauts must also keep the ISS in good condition and make repairs as needed. This can sometimes require spacewalking or the use of cutting-edge technology. Though their area is confined and conditions can be risky, astronauts aboard the ISS conduct some pretty groundbreaking work.

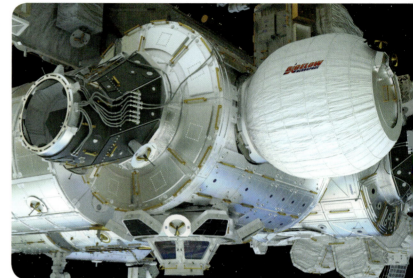

PROJECT BEAM

Looking toward an eventual space mission to Mars, astronauts are testing the durability of a structure called the Bigelow Expandable Activity Module (BEAM). It has the potential to provide space for people to live and work on the Red Planet. Space habitats must be lightweight and easy to build, and they must perform in microgravity and the vacuum of space. They also need to protect against solar radiation and space debris. A BEAM would take less precious room on a rocket but provide greatly enhanced living and working space when expanded.

The expanded BEAM attached to the ISS

A SOCIAL EXPERIMENT

For one space experiment, researchers asked 10 astronauts to journal their experiences aboard the space station at least three times per week. Most of their entries related to topics of work, communication with people on Earth, adjustment to their environment, social interaction, how they spent their free time, equipment, events, organization/management, sleep, and food. Researchers were able to draw some interesting conclusions on human behavior from the astronauts' entries since social issues tend to intensify when a small group works within a confined space.

Astronauts Terry Virts, Samantha Cristoforetti, and Barry "Butch" Wilmore (left to right)

ROBONAUT

A robot with a human form stands ready to help with projects around the ISS. Ground operators can control it remotely and onboard crew members can operate it by wearing a vest, special gloves, and a 3-D visor. All the crew members have to do is make the same movements they want the robot to make. This new space friend can perform some of the riskier tasks and give the astronauts a break.

NASA astronaut Catherine "Cady" Coleman poses with Robonaut 2

Spacewalks

Any time an astronaut leaves a space vehicle while still in space, it's referred to as a spacewalk or extravehicular activity (EVA). Astronauts go on spacewalks to perform science experiments, test new equipment, or repair satellites and spacecraft.

Before leaving the spacecraft, an astronaut must first put on his spacesuit and breathe pure oxygen for two hours. This gets the nitrogen out of his system, which could cause gas bubbles to form in his blood. The gas bubbles cause debilitating physical problems called the "bends."

When spacewalking, the astronaut's spacesuit provides him with air and water. He tethers his tools to his spacesuit and tethers himself to the spacecraft to keep both him and his tools from floating away into space. He also stays safe by wearing a SAFER, a Simplified Aid for EVA Rescue. It has jet thrusters to help the astronaut control his movements in space during emergencies. He can control the SAFER with a small joystick.

WetLab-2 Studies

WetLab-2, a new research platform aboard the ISS, allows biologists to perform gene activity analysis and other research in the microgravity of space. This will help researchers rapidly identify changes in astronauts' gene expression, with the goal of lessening the harmful effects of long-duration spaceflight.

Did you know?

Astronauts train for spacewalks in a large swimming pool because floating in space is a lot like floating in water. They also practice by enacting a spacewalk with a virtual reality simulation.

European Space Agency (ESA) astronaut Christer Fuglesang

NASA Astronaut Col. Jeffrey Williams

Much of the work astronauts are currently doing will advance the international space program's long-term goals. Veteran astronauts like Col. Jeff Williams are laying the foundation for future missions—including one planned for Mars.

Col. Williams is the first American to be a long-term resident of the ISS for three separate expeditions. He has taken more photos from space than anyone else—well over 330,000. During his expeditions he has conducted hundreds of experiments related to plants, animals, cells, DNA, physics, and other areas. He has also taken several spacewalks. He was the first to interact live with social media followers while in space and posted to social media almost daily about his experiences, work, and photos from the ISS.

"I don't find a conflict with true science—genuine science with integrity—and the Scriptures. I have found that in all cases where there is a conflict, it's not a conflict with the science, it's a conflict with the presupposition going in."[7]

—Astronaut Col. Jeffrey N. Williams

Searching for Life

After Charles Darwin popularized the theory of evolution, people began to wonder if life could have evolved on other planets. The question soon surfaced, "Are we alone?"

With the advent of radio in the early 20th century, scientists began using sound waves to search the cosmos for signs of other sound waves indicating intelligent life. The Bible doesn't tell us that God created life anywhere else, and none has ever been discovered outside of Earth. However, studying other planets has benefits. When we explore the universe, we learn more about God's wonderful creation.

SETI

The search for extraterrestrial intelligence (SETI) is the general name given for the search for other life forms in the universe. It's a global effort by many different people and organizations. Many scientists, including Stephen Hawking and Carl Sagan, have emphasized the importance of SETI. Telescopes have been built with both private and government funds, countless signals have been sent out, and many hours of listening have occurred. But so far we haven't received any definitive sign of extraterrestrial intelligence.

FERMI PARADOX

In the 1950s, Italian physicist Enrico Fermi reasoned that if the universe is old and life can evolve from non-life, then technologically advanced cultures should be common and easily detectable.

Enrico Fermi

So why haven't we detected any outside of our planet? This lack of observational evidence led Fermi to ask, "Where is everybody?" This question became known as the Fermi paradox, also referred to as the Great Silence.

EXOPLANETS

An exoplanet is simply a terrestrial planet that orbits a star outside our solar system. So far, secular scientists have estimated the existence of trillions of exoplanets. NASA and many other institutions are trying to determine if any of them are suitable for life.

NECESSARY FOR LIFE

Conditions must be just right for a planet to sustain life. These include:

- A star like our sun that's neither too cold nor too hot.
- An exoplanet orbiting in the habitable zone of a star.
- An exoplanet roughly the size of Earth.
- An exoplanet with an atmosphere of ozone, oxygen, and water.

THE HABITABLE ZONE

The habitable zone, also known as the *Goldilocks* zone, is an area around a main sequence yellow dwarf star that provides life-sustaining temperatures—like where Earth orbits. The right temperatures support the presence of liquid water on a planet. Too close to the star and water would boil. Too far and it would freeze.

THE RIGHT SIZE

An exoplanet must be roughly the size of Earth to support life. If it weren't, its gravity would be too strong and destroy life or too weak and fail to hold an atmosphere.

WATER IN SPACE

Scientists have found evidence of mostly frozen water on Mars, Jupiter, Saturn, Uranus, Neptune, Pluto, and asteroids and comets. The water molecule H_2O is fairly common in the universe, but *liquid* water is rare—except on Earth. Much evidence indicates that Mars has sustained massive catastrophic flooding even though it has no liquid water today.

THE PERFECT STAR

A habitable exoplanet requires a star like our sun: a main sequence yellow dwarf. These stars are quite common, but not all of them are stable. Life needs a star that is neither too hot nor too cold, and stable enough to allow life to grow and flourish on an orbiting planet.

CAN LIFE EVOLVE?

Even if another planet had the right environment to sustain life, it doesn't mean that life could naturally evolve there. Though oxygen, water, and minerals support cellular life, they attack the basic molecules inside cells that are not already part of a living being. That means that living cells could not have developed from non-living chemicals.

"The Spirit of God has made me, and the breath of the Almighty gives me life." (Job 33:4)

God's Attributes Are Clearly Seen

The Bible tells us that "the heavens declare the glory of God" (Psalm 19:1) and His attributes are "clearly seen" by all that He has made (Romans 1:20). So what does the universe reveal about our divine Creator?

How Does God Provide and Protect?

When we list the many ways God provides for us each day, we realize how gracious He is to us. God made the sun that gives us light to see and warmth to function, and grows our food to supply us with nutrients. His Earth brings forth vegetation for our food, and the water cycle helps satisfy our thirst. He gave Earth the atmosphere and magnetic field that shield us from harmful solar radiation and space debris. He created the moon, which provides us with gentle light in the night, keeps our oceans from stagnating, protects us from many of the space rocks that cross our planet's path, and prevents Earth from tilting too far from the attraction of the sun or Jupiter. God provides for and protects His creation.

How Creative Is He?

The variety of colors, patterns, textures, luminosities, orbits, and other unique characteristics of celestial bodies throughout the universe show God's affinity for diversity. Everything in creation could be gray and dull, but that wouldn't reflect His multifaceted nature. The tilt of the earth as it orbits the sun brings seasons with golden leaves, spring blossoms, winter frost, and warm summer beaches. Each one provides its own joys and benefits. God made each planet with its own hidden mysteries, raw beauty, and breathtaking views, and stars in the sky display a wide range of color and intensity. The whole world reveals God's creativity.

What about Life?

The way God orchestrated the universe to make Earth a suitable place for people and animals shows that He intends for life to thrive here. He placed Earth at the perfect location within our solar system to avoid the extreme temperatures, toxic gases, wrong air pressures, lack of food and water, and dangerous radiation that make all other planets so far studied completely unsuitable for life. Earth's life-friendliness showcases God's love for life, "for in Him we live and move and have our being" (Acts 17:28).

KNOWLEDGE AND WISDOM

We can see glimpses of God's infinite wisdom when we study our well-ordered universe. Each celestial body serves a purpose in its current position and orbit. God positioned our solar system to avoid collisions with other stars and to be protected from harmful radiation found far outside our solar system. His precise balance between angular momentum and gravity keeps celestial bodies in their places.

"Now to the King eternal, immortal, invisible, to God who alone is wise, be honor and glory forever and ever. Amen." (1 Timothy 1:17)

UNLIMITED POWER

The enormous measures of energy in our universe require a power source so great that "infinite" is the best word we have to describe it. Only a supernatural Creator with infinite power could have created this universe. Scientists estimate that billions of galaxies exist, each one with solar systems, stars, planets, and other celestial bodies. How vast must His power be that His spoken word brought them all into being?

"You are worthy, O Lord, to receive glory and honor and power; for You created all things, and by Your will they exist and were created."
(Revelation 4:11)

HOW HE LOVES US

We see God's love not only in what He has made but also in what He has done for us through His Son, Jesus. As amazing as this universe is, it still suffers under sin's Curse pronounced in Genesis 3. This sin invades every part of creation—especially humanity.

Yet, our Creator loved us so much that He supplied a way for us to be redeemed from this Curse. He performed the greatest act of love when He came to Earth in the form of a man, the Lord Jesus Christ, who lived a sinless life, died unjustly at the hands of His own creation, and rose from the grave. His death served as payment for our sinful hearts and actions, and His resurrection allows us to live new lives in Him.

For all who accept our Creator's invitation, He promises a new heavens and new Earth. That new place will be more than we can imagine, and we can then say goodbye once and for all to sin, sickness, and tears. We will know Him fully as we are also known, and we will reign with Him forever in a new world that never grows old.

The universe reveals attributes of a God bigger than we could ever dream of. Every moment of life and breath presents an opportunity to worship Him, and we can reflect His nature by providing for others, protecting life, creatively ministering to others, making wise decisions, using our power for good, and loving those whom God brings into our paths.

"For God so loved the world that He gave His only begotten Son, that whoever believes in Him should not perish but have everlasting life." (John 3:16)

Index

air pressure, 92-93, 108

Alpha Centauri, 21

Andromeda galaxy, 70-71

antimatter problem, 23

antiproton, 23

Apollo 11; 52, 78, 88-89

Apollo 13; 89

Ariel, 47

Aristotle, 12-14

Armstrong, Neil; 78, 88-89

artificial intelligence, 97

asteroid(s), 26, 28, 41, 66-67, 82-83, 94, 98, 107

astronaut(s), 40-41, 52, 64, 79, 82, 84, 86, 88-93, 98-102, 104-105

astronomer(s), 12-13, 20-22, 27-28, 32, 37, 43, 46, 48-51, 54, 56-57, 60-62, 64-68, 70-71, 74, 80

astronomical unit(s)/AU(s), 20-21, 36

asymmetry problem, 23

atmosphere, 10, 30-32, 37, 39-41, 44-46, 49, 52, 61, 64, 66, 75, 82, 85, 87-89, 92, 94-95, 99, 107-108

atmospheric pressure, 32, 37, 40-41, 91

auroras, 45, 52

barred spiral galaxy(ies), 71

Big Bang, 11, 22-24, 62, 65, 72-73

Bigelow Expandable Activity Module (BEAM), 104

binary stars, 65

black hole(s), 19, 24, 55, 65, 68-69, 71

blue star(s), 54, 56-57, 75

Callisto, 43

Cassini, 45, 83

centaur(s), 26, 66-67

Ceres, 66

Charon, 50

chromosphere, 29

comet(s), 10, 26, 28, 46, 61, 66-67, 73, 75, 82, 86, 94, 107

constellation(s), 12, 56, 60

convection zone, 29

Copernican Revolution, 13-14

Copernicus, Nicolaus; 13-15

corona, 29

cosmic microwave background radiation (CMB), 22-23

cosmological principle, 22

cosmology(ies), 14-15, 19, 24-25, 65

crater(s), 30-31, 33, 36, 39, 41, 45, 51, 83

creation, 8-12, 20, 22, 24-27, 37, 43, 45, 47-49, 51-53, 63-64, 67, 73-75, 83, 86, 106, 108-109

Creator, 8, 11, 28, 33, 72-73, 108-109

dark matter, 72

dark energy, 72

Darwin, Charles; 106

Deimos, 41

diameter, 12, 20, 26, 28, 38, 40-42, 46, 49-51, 71, 85

distant starlight, 22, 62

Dragon, 98, 103

dwarf planet(s), 21, 26-27, 50-51, 75, 79, 87

dwarf star(s), 10, 54-55, 68, 107

dynamo theory, 53

Eagle, 52, 88-89

Earth, 8-15, 17, 19-21, 25-34, 36-46, 48-54, 57, 60-64, 66, 69, 71, 75, 78-79, 82-84, 86-89, 92-96, 98-101, 104, 106-109

eclipse(s), 11-12, 28-29, 38-39, 61

ecliptic, 26, 37

Einstein, Albert; 18-19, 25, 63, 69

ellipse, 17, 26

elliptical galaxies, 70

Enceladus, 45, 75, 83

energy, 18-19, 22, 24-25, 28-29, 32, 36-38, 42, 49, 53, 56, 62, 72, 74-75, 96, 109

Eris, 51

Europa, 43

European Space Agency (ESA), 35, 83, 105

event horizon, 55, 69

evolution, 33, 106

exoplanet(s), 36, 106-107

expansion, 22-23, 25, 72

Explorer 1; 94

extravehicular activity (EVA), 105

Extravehicular Mobility Unit (EMU), 93

Fermi paradox, 106

Fermi, Enrico; 106

firmament, 9-11, 63

flatness problem, 22-23

galaxy(ies), 10, 19-22, 25, 55-56, 62-64, 68-72, 80-81, 96, 109

galaxy cluster, 64, 71

Galilean satellites, 43

Galilei, Galileo; 13-15, 43, 48, 70

Galileo (spacecraft), 43, 83

Ganymede, 43, 45

gas giants, 26, 51

general theory of relativity, 18-19, 69

geocentrism, 12-15, 43

geyser(s), 45, 49, 75, 83

giants (stars), 55

Goldilocks zone, 107

gravity, 22, 24, 26-27, 31, 36, 38, 40-42, 48, 54, 57, 68, 72, 79, 92, 99, 107, 109

Great Attractor, 71

Great Dark Spot, 49

Great Red Spot, 42, 49

Great Silence, 106

greatest elongation, 31

Hadfield, Chris; 92

Halley's Comet, 86

Hartnett, John; 25

Hawking, Stephen; 106

heaven(s), 9-12, 14, 20, 25, 34, 39, 58, 63-64, 80, 108-109

heliocentrism, 13-15, 43

helium, 26, 28-29, 44, 46, 49, 56, 65

Herschel, William; 46

holography, 96

Hooke, Robert; 16-17

horizon problem, 22-23, 62

Hubble Space Telescope, 45, 49-50, 79-81, 84, 95

Hubble, Edwin, 22, 80

human(s), 8, 12, 15, 37, 40, 46, 51, 54, 63, 70, 78, 81, 92-93, 96-99, 104, 109

Humphreys, Russell; 25, 47, 52-53, 75, 83

Hydra, 50

hydrogen, 26, 28-29, 44, 46, 49, 54, 56-57, 65, 68, 75, 85, 99

hyperdrive, 96

inflation, 23, 73

International Space Station (ISS), 79, 84, 91-93, 98-102, 104

Io, 43, 74

irregular galaxy(ies), 71

Jupiter, 15, 26-28, 42-43, 45-49, 53, 66-67, 74, 79, 83, 87, 107-108

Kelly, Mark; 93

Kelly, Scott; 91-93

Kepler 438b, 36

Kepler, Johannes; 26

Kerberos, 50

$$\mathcal{E} = mc^2$$

Kuiper Belt, 67

Laniakea Supercluster, 71

laws of motion, 16-17

laws of physics, 8, 19, 55, 73

light(s), 9-11, 16, 19, 22-25, 28-29, 36, 38, 46, 50, 52, 54-55, 60-64, 68-70, 80, 95-97, 108

lightsabers, 97, 101

light speed, 19, 22, 25, 63, 96-97

light-year(s), 20-21, 55, 62, 70-71, 86-87, 96

Lisle, Jason; 25, 63

Lowell, Percival; 51

Luna 2; 89

Magellan, 33, 83

magnetic field(s), 18, 29-31, 37, 42, 45, 47, 49, 52-54, 57, 75, 83, 108

magnetic pole(s), 23

magnetic shield, 36

main sequence star(s), 28, 54-55

Mariner 10; 30-31, 52, 75, 83

Mars, 26-27, 36, 40-41, 50, 66, 78, 82-83, 93, 98, 104-105, 107

matter, 18, 22-25, 65, 68-69, 72, 96

Mercury, 26-27, 30-31, 36, 43, 47, 52-53, 75, 83, 87

Messenger, 31, 52, 75, 83

meteor, 61

meteorite(s), 10, 44

microgravity, 79, 92, 99-101, 104-105

Milky Way, 20-21, 29, 68, 70-71

Miranda, 47

monopole problem, 22-23

moon (Earth's), 8, 10-13, 21, 29-30, 33, 38-41, 45, 58, 60-61, 67, 78, 84, 86-89, 94, 98, 108

moon(s), 9, 15, 28, 32, 39, 41, 43-45, 47, 49-50, 64, 74-75, 82-83, 87, 94

multiverse, 23, 73

National Aeronautics and Space Administration (NASA), 21, 30-31, 33, 44, 48, 52, 78, 80-81, 84-85, 88-93, 95, 100-101, 104-106

naturalists, 72, 83

naturalistic, 8, 28, 49, 55, 57, 65, 72-73, 83

nebula(e), 28, 33, 54, 57, 65, 81

Neptune, 26-27, 48-51, 53, 67, 79, 83, 107

New General Catalogue (NGC), 46

New Horizons, 21, 50-51, 75, 79, 82-83

Newton, Isaac; 16-17, 26, 48

nitrogen, 49, 75, 84, 105

Nix, 50

nuclear fusion, 28-29, 54, 56

Oberon, 47

ocean(s), 33, 37-38, 85, 88, 95, 108

Olympus Mons, 40

Oort cloud, 67, 73

origin(s), 8, 22, 24, 39, 41, 53, 56, 74

Orion, 56, 60, 71

Pale Blue Dot, 36-37, 83

parallax, 21

parsec(s), 20-21

Phobos, 41

photosphere, 29

plate tectonics, 37

Plato, 12-14

Pluto, 21, 27, 50-51, 75, 78-79, 82-83, 87, 107

probe(s), 33, 78-79, 82-83, 88-89, 94

Ptolemy, 13-15, 60

Puck, 47

quasar(s), 22, 25, 65

radiation, 22-23, 29, 36-37, 45, 52, 69, 72, 75, 92, 104, 108-109

radiative zone, 29

ray guns, 97

recession, 38

retrograde orbit, 49

ring(s), 32, 43-47, 49, 53, 74

rocket(s), 78, 80, 84-85, 88, 91, 95, 104

rover, 41, 78, 82-83

Sagan, Carl; 106

satellite(s), 13, 19, 43, 79-80, 82, 84, 94-95, 105

Saturn, 26-27, 43-46, 48, 53, 55, 74-75, 79, 83, 107

search for extraterrestrial intelligence (SETI), 106

seasons, 8-9, 32, 37-38, 40-41, 60, 108

shuttle(s), 33, 79, 84-85, 93

Simplified Aid For EVA Rescue (SAFER), 105

Skylab, 79

solar eclipse, 12, 28-29, 38

solar radiation, 75, 92, 104, 108

solar system(s), 13-14, 20-21, 26-28, 30-33, 36, 39-40, 42-48, 50-53, 65-67, 69-71, 73-75, 79, 82-83, 87, 106, 108-109

solar wind, 52, 82, 94

Soyuz, 91

space junk, 95

Space Race, 78, 94, 98

spacesuit(s), 40, 93, 105

spacewalk(s), 78, 93, 100, 104-105

SpaceX, 98

speed of light, 19, 22, 25, 63, 96-97

spiral galaxy(ies), 56, 70-72, 81

Sputnik 1; 82, 94

star classification, 54

star composition, 54

star formation, 54-57

Styx, 50

sun, 8-14, 20-21, 26-33, 36-51, 54-57, 60-61, 66-68, 71, 73, 75, 87, 93-95, 107-108

sunspots, 29

supergiants, 10, 55

supernova(s), 54, 56-57, 63, 65, 68, 75

teleportation, 96

terrestrial planet(s), 26, 32-33, 36, 51, 106

tidal locking, 39, 50

tilt(s), 32-33, 37-38, 41, 44, 47, 50, 87, 108

time, 8-9, 11, 19-20, 22, 25, 55, 62-63, 69, 96

Titan, 45, 75, 83

Titania, 47

Tombaugh, Clyde; 50-51, 83

trans-Neptunian object (TNO), 26, 50-51

Triton, 48-49

Trojan asteroids, 66

Trojan moons, 45

Umbriel, 47

Uranus, 26-27, 46-51, 53, 66, 79, 83, 87, 107

Venus, 26-27, 31-33, 36, 42, 66, 74, 82-83, 87

Virgo Supercluster, 71

volcano(es), 32-33, 37, 40, 43, 74

Voyager 1; 36, 83

Voyager 2; 46-49, 53, 79, 83

water, 36-38, 40-41, 46, 53, 74-75, 88, 91, 99-100, 105, 107-108

white dwarf(s), 55, 68

white hole(s), 24-25

Williams, Jeffrey (Jeff); 91, 101-102, 105

worldview(s), 8, 33, 36, 67

wormholes, 19, 96

Wright, Thomas; 70

Z-2 spacesuit, 93

Contributors

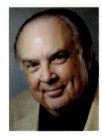

Henry M. Morris III, D. Min.
Chief Executive Officer

Dr. Henry M. Morris III holds four earned degrees, including a D.Min. from Luther Rice Seminary and the Presidents and Key Executives MBA from Pepperdine University. A former college professor, administrator, business executive, and senior pastor, Dr. Morris is an articulate and passionate speaker frequently invited to address church congregations, college assemblies, and national conferences. The eldest son of ICR's founder, Dr. Morris has served for many years in conference and writing ministry. His love for the Word of God and passion for Christian maturity, coupled with God's gift of teaching, have given Dr. Morris a broad and effective ministry over the years. He has authored numerous articles and books, including *The Big Three, Exploring the Evidence for Creation, 5 Reasons to Believe in Recent Creation, The Book of Beginnings, Pulling Down Strongholds, A Firm Foundation, Six Days of Creation, Your Origins Matter,* and *Unlocking the Mysteries of Genesis.* He is also a contributor to *Guide to Creation Basics* and *Creation Basics & Beyond* and is the featured speaker in *Creation: A Bible Basic* (DVD) and *Geology and the Great Flood* (DVD).

Jason Lisle, Ph.D., Astrophysics

Dr. Jason Lisle graduated *summa cum laude* from Ohio Wesleyan University, where he double-majored in physics and astronomy and minored in mathematics. He earned a master's degree and a Ph.D. in astrophysics at the University of Colorado. Dr. Lisle specialized in solar astrophysics and has made a number of scientific discoveries regarding the solar photosphere and has contributed to the field of general relativity. After completion of his research at the University of Colorado, Dr. Lisle began working in full-time apologetics ministry, focusing on the defense of Genesis. Dr. Lisle was instrumental in developing the planetarium at the Creation Museum in Kentucky, writing and directing planetarium shows including "The Created Cosmos." Dr. Lisle speaks on topics related to science and the defense of the Christian faith. He has authored numerous articles and books demonstrating that biblical creation is the only logical possibility for origins. His books include *Understanding Genesis, The Ultimate Proof of Creation, Discerning Truth, The Stargazer's Guide to the Night Sky, Taking Back Astronomy,* and *The Solar System: God's Heavenly Handiwork.* He is also a contributor to *Guide to Creation Basics* and *Creation Basics & Beyond,* and he is the featured speaker in *The Secret Code of Creation* (DVD).

Jake Hebert, Ph.D., Physics

Dr. Jake Hebert earned a master's degree in physics in 1999 from Texas A&M University, where he studied optics and was a Dean's Graduate Fellow 1995-1996. He received his Ph.D. in 2011 from the University of Texas at Dallas, where his research involved a study of the possible connection between fair-weather atmospheric electricity and weather and climate. He has taught at both the high school and university levels. He joined ICR in 2011 as a research associate and focuses much of his work on climates before and after Noah's Flood, among other research endeavors. He has written numerous articles for *Acts & Facts* and technical journals. He is the author of *The Ice Age and the Flood* and a contributor to *Guide to Creation Basics* and *Creation Basics & Beyond.* He is the featured speaker in *The Ice Age: Real and Recent* (DVD).

Brian Thomas, M.S., Biotechnology

Brian Thomas received his bachelor's degree in biology in 1993 and a master's in biotechnology in 1999 from Stephen F. Austin State University. He taught junior high and high school as well as biology, chemistry, and anatomy as an adjunct and assistant professor at Dallas-area universities. Since 2008, Mr. Thomas has been a science writer and editor at ICR, where he contributes news and magazine articles, speaks on creation issues, and researches original tissue fossils. In this book, he wrote the segment "What Does the Bible Say about Space?," adapted segments of "Starlight and Time," and reviewed and edited the entire manuscript. He is the author of *Dinosaurs and the Bible* and a contributor to *Guide to Creation Basics, Creation Basics & Beyond, Guide to Dinosaurs,* and *Guide to the Human Body.* He is also the featured speaker in *Discovering Dinosaurs: Five Details from Fossils and History* (DVD).

Susan Windsor, Graphic Designer at ICR, provided design, layout, and artistic expertise. She also designed *Guide to Creation Basics, Guide to Animals, Guide to Dinosaurs, Guide to the Human Body, Unlocking the Mysteries of Genesis Viewer Guide* and *Student Guide, Made in His Image Viewer Guide, Uncovering the Truth about Dinosaurs Viewer Guide,* and other ICR publications.

Susan Windsor   Jayme Durant

Jayme Durant, Director of Communications and Executive Editor at ICR, developed the *Guide to…* series concept and content throughout this book. She also developed the concepts and content for *Guide to Creation Basics, Guide to Animals, Guide to Dinosaurs, Guide to the Human Body, Unlocking the Mysteries of Genesis Viewer Guide* and *Student Guide, Made in His Image Viewer Guide, Uncovering the Truth about Dinosaurs Viewer Guide,* and other ICR publications. She worked with AMS/Alchemy to develop content and scripts for the following ICR DVD series: *Unlocking the Mysteries of Genesis, Made in His Image,* and *Uncovering the Truth about Dinosaurs.*

Christy Hardy   Truett Billups

Christy Hardy, Editor and staff writer at ICR, worked closely with Jayme Durant in developing the content throughout the book, using research from ICR scientists and scholars. Hardy developed every segment into the existing format. She also wrote and/or adapted and edited the following segments: "Origins of an Orchestrated Universe"; "Jupiter, a Giant Jewel"; "Celebrating Saturn"; "Caution: Astronauts at Work"; and "God's Attributes Are Clearly Seen." Hardy contributed to *Guide to the Human Body, Made in His Image Viewer Guide,* and *Uncovering the Truth about Dinosaurs Viewer Guide.*

Michael Stamp   Beth Mull

Truett Billups, Editor and staff writer at ICR, wrote and/or adapted and edited the following segments: "Astronomers in History"; "The Copernican Revolution"; "Isaac Newton, Father of Physics"; "The Achievements of Albert Einstein"; "Melting on Mercury"; "Magnetic Fields and Why They Matter"; "Studying the Stars"; "Stargazing Basics for Beginners"; "Asteroids, Comets, and Other Celestial Mysteries"; "Gazing at Galaxies"; "Naturalistic Speculations"; "Evidence for a Young Universe"; "NASA's Intriguing History"; "A Tribute to the Hubble Space Telescope"; "The Space Shuttle Program"; "Fascinating Space Facts"; "Man on the Moon"; "How to Be an Astronaut"; "The Human Body in Space"; "Science Fiction vs. Reality"; "Building the International Space Station"; "Life on the International Space Station"; and "Searching for Life." Billups also contributed to *Guide to the Human Body, Noah's Ark: Adventures on Ararat, Made in His Image Viewer Guide,* and *Uncovering the Truth about Dinosaurs Viewer Guide.*

Michael Stamp, Editor and staff writer at ICR, wrote and/or adapted and edited the following segments: "How Big Is Our Universe?"; "Origins of the Big Bang"; "Creation Cosmologies"; "Our Perfectly Balanced Solar System"; "The Sun: Supporting Life on Earth"; "Venus, Earth's Sister Planet"; "Our Extraordinary Earth"; "The Making of the Moon"; "Mysterious Mars"; "Unexpected Uranus"; "Neptune, Blue as the Sea"; "Pluto, the Dwarf Planet"; "Blue Stars and Star Formation"; "Starlight and Time"; "Outer Space and Other Marvels"; "Shedding Light on Black Holes"; "Exploring Space Probes"; and "Sending Out Satellites." Stamp also contributed to *Guide to the Human Body.*

Beth Mull, Senior Editor and staff writer for ICR, provided editorial expertise throughout this book. She has edited *Acts & Facts, Days of Praise,* web content, *Book of Beginnings, Guide to Creation Basics, Guide to Animals, Guide to Dinosaurs,* and many other ICR publications. Mull also contributed to and edited *Guide to the Human Body.*

Acknowledgment

Col. Jeffrey Williams, NASA astronaut and International Space Station (ISS) commander

Special thanks to Col. Jeffrey Williams for providing interviews, allowing us to spend time with him at NASA, answering questions from the ISS, meeting ICR in a private videoconference during his extended stay at the ISS, and even reviewing some portions of this book while in space—wow! He returned to Earth September 6, 2016, completing a five-and-a-half month mission with Expedition 47/48's crew. He set the record for the most cumulative days in space by a NASA astronaut, with 534 total days over four missions. Bold about his faith, he often quotes Scripture in his social media posts. In the videoconference with ICR, he mentioned his deep admiration for God's providence. He sees how God has worked throughout his life, eventually preparing him to be where he is now as an astronaut. In addition to being an ISS commander, he has also taken over 330,000 pictures from space. His brief NASA biography touches on his incredible accomplishments: "A West Point graduate, Col. Williams received his commission as a second lieutenant in 1980 and was designated an Army aviator in 1981. He earned a Master of Science Degree in Aeronautical Engineering and the Degree of Aeronautical Engineer from the U.S. Naval Postgraduate School in 1987. Col. Williams graduated first in U.S. Naval Test Pilot School class 103 in 1993. He earned a second graduate degree, Master of Arts Degree in National Security and Strategic Studies from the U.S. Naval War College in 1996. Williams was selected for the NASA Astronaut Class of 1996. Williams retired from active [military] duty in 2007 after more than 27 years of service. His special honors and awards are almost too numerous to list."[8] While these achievements are impressive, there's even more to this remarkable man. It's been inspiring to follow along with him on his journey in space and see the glory of God's creation through his eyes. Many thanks for his insight into God's creative handiwork displayed throughout our incredible universe!

Publication Credits

Portions of this book were adapted from the following sources.

Coppedge, D. 2008. Rescuing Ring Ages. *Acts & Facts*. 37 (10): 15.

Lisle, J. 2012. Blue Stars Confirm Recent Creation. *Acts & Facts*. 41 (9): 16

Lisle, J. 2013. The Solar System: The Sun. *Acts & Facts*. 42 (7): 10-12.

Lisle, J. 2013. The Solar System: Mercury. *Acts & Facts*. 42 (8): 10-12.

Lisle, J. 2013. The Solar System: Venus. *Acts & Facts*. 42 (9): 10-12.

Lisle, J. 2013. The Solar System: Earth and Moon. *Acts & Facts*. 42 (10): 10-12.

Lisle, J. 2013. The Solar System: Mars. *Acts & Facts*. 42 (11): 10-12.

Lisle, J. 2013. The Solar System: Jupiter. *Acts & Facts*. 42 (12): 10-12.

Lisle, J. 2014. The Solar System: Saturn. *Acts & Facts*. 43 (1): 10-12.

Lisle, J. 2014. The Solar System: Uranus. *Acts & Facts*. 43 (2): 10-12.

Lisle, J. 2014. The Solar System: Neptune. *Acts & Facts*. 43 (3): 10-12.

Lisle, J. 2014. The Solar System: Pluto. *Acts & Facts*. 43 (4): 10-12.

Lisle, J. 2014. The Solar System: Asteroids and Comets. *Acts & Facts*. 43 (5): 12-15.

Endnotes

1. Morris III, H. 2009. *Exploring the Evidence for Creation*. Eugene, OR: Harvest House Publishers, 31.

2. Lisle, J. 2012. *The Stargazer's Guide to the Night Sky*. Green Forest, AR: Master Books, 33.

3. Ibid, 39.

4. Cupps, V. R. Scientific Suicide. *Creation Science Update*. Posted on ICR.org May 4, 2015.

5. Howell, E. Earth Living Is Tough for Astronaut Used to Space. *Space.com*. Posted on space.com June 3, 2013.

6. No Author. 2015. Above All the Earth. *Acts & Facts*. 44 (3): 6.

7. Ibid, 5.

8. Astronaut Biography: Jeffrey N. Williams. Posted on jsc.nasa.gov.

Image Credits

t-top; m-middle; b-bottom;
c-center; l-left; r-right

Bigelow Aerospace: 104tr

Bigstock: 8, 9 (except ml), 10-11, 12tr, bl, br, 14r, 15m, r, 17tl, bl, br, 19b, 20, 22tr, 24, 26l, 28ml, mr, r, 29, 30tl, m, 33t, 36b, 37-38, 39t, 42tr, 48bl, 52tr, 53b, 56tr, 57b, 60, 61t, br, 62, 63r, 64b, 66-67b, 70tr, 71br, 72-73, 80tr, 86tr, b, 87mbl, bl, br, 90l, r, 95t, m, 96-97, 106t, bl, 107tr, mr, b, 108-109

Rita Greer (via Wikipedia): 16br

European Space Agency (ESA): 23tl, 54mr, 66bl

ESA-Hubble & NASA: 25r, 65tr, 81tr

ESA-Hubble & NASA/Judy Schmidt: 9ml

ESA-Hubble & NASA/R. Buta (University of Alabama): 54bl

ESA-Hubble & NASA/Serge Meunier: 54bl

ESA/NASA: 34-35

Fotolia: 76-77

ICR: 27t, 30b, 50m, 53ml

MPIA/NASA, Calar Alto Observatory: 56bl

NASA: 21tr, 22br, 26bmr, br, 27br, 31ml, tr, mr, 33mr, 39b, 40tr, 41tr, mtr, 43tl, 45br, 46bl, 47tr, m, 49tl, tm, br, 51br, 52br, 64tr, 65m, 69tr, 78, 79tl, bl, 80bl, 82b, 83mr, 84-85, 86tl, 87tml, 88-89, 90bl, 92-93, 94t, 98-99, 100tl, b, 101, 104m, b, 105

NASA/Aubrey Gemignani: 91m

NASA/Bill Ingalls: 91l, r

NASA, ESA, and A. Simon (Goddard Space Flight Center): 53tm

NASA, ESA, and J. Lotz, STScI and the HFF team: 71ml

NASA, ESA, and the HST Frontier Fields Team, STSc Acknowledgement Judy Schmidt: 21b

NASA, ESA, and the Hubble Heritage Team, STScI, AURA: 55t, 58-59, 70m, 71m, 81tr, br

NASA, ESA, J. Hester, Arizona State University: 57t, 65br

NASA/ISS: 102-103

NASA/Johns Hopkins University Applied Physics Laboratory/Carnegie Institution of Washington: 26bl, 30tr, 31b, 32mr, 52ml

NASA/Johns Hopkins University Applied Physics Laboratory/Southwest Research Institute: 50tr, b, 51bl, 75b, 79br, 87tm

NASA/Johnson Space Center: 100tr

NASA/JPL: 27bm, 32bl, 33b, 40ml, 41m, 44bl, 46tr, 49tr, bl, 74tl, b, 79tr

NASA/JPL, Caltech: 36tr, 42bl, 47bm, 53tr, 55br, 61bl, 68, 71tr, 83bl

NASA/JPL, Caltech, Cornell University, Arizona State University: 40-41b

NASA/JPL, Caltech, Space Science Institute: 45bl

NASA/JPL, Caltech, UCLA: 22bl

NASA/JPL, Caltech, UMD: 67tr

NASA/JPL, Caltech, University of Arizona: 41mbr

NASA/JPL, Cornell University, Maas Digital LLC: 82t

NASA/JPL/DLR: 43ml

NASA/JPL/DLR, German Aerospace Center: 43m

NASA/JPL, Space Science Institute: 27bl, 44t, 45m, 53m, 75tl, tr, 83br, 87mr

NASA/JPL, University of Arizona: 43br

NASA/JPL, University of Arizona, PIRL: 74mr

NASA/JPL, University of Arizona, University of Idaho: 45tr

NASA/JPL/USGS: 48tr

NASA and M. Weiss, Chandra X-ray Center: 69b

NASA/MSFC, Jacobs Technology, ESSSA, Aaron Kingery: 75m

NASA/NOAA/GOES Project: 26bm, 36mr, 52m, 87tl, 107m

NASA/NSSDC: 94b

NASA/SDO: 28bl

NASA/SSV, MIPL, Magellan Team: 26bml, 32tr, 87tr

NASA/STSci: 51mr

NASA/Swift, Stefan Immler, GSFC, and Erin Grand, UMCP: 70b

Niko Lang (via Wikipedia): 14bl

NOAA: 95b

Public domain: 12tl, 13, 14m, 15bl, 16tr, bl, 17tr, 18, 19tr, 22tl, 26tr, 43tr, 48ml, bm, 51tm, tr, 54ml, 63bl, 67tl, 69tl, 70tl, 80br, 106br

Paul Wiegert, University of Western Ontario Canada: 66tr

About the Institute for Creation Research

Founded by Dr. Henry Morris in 1970, ICR exists to conduct scientific research within the realms of origins and Earth history and to educate through training programs, conferences, media presentations, and print resources. ICR was established for three main purposes:

Research. ICR conducts laboratory, field, and theoretical research on projects that seek to understand the science of origins and Earth history. ICR scientists have conducted numerous research projects in various locations and on vital issues such as Radioisotopes and the Age of the Earth (RATE), Flood-Activated Sedimentation and Tectonics (FAST), the human genome, distant starlight, geological effects of the Flood, dinosaur proteins, paleoclimatology, organism interface, and much more.

Dr. Henry Morris

Education. ICR offers courses and seminars that train men and women to do real-world apologetics with a foundation of biblical authority and creation science. ICR also offers a one-year, non-degree training program called the Creationist Worldview.

Communication. ICR produces books, videos, periodicals, and other media to communicate its research findings and related information. ICR's main publication is *Acts & Facts,* a free full-color magazine with a readership of more than 250,000, and its website ICR.org features regular and relevant creation science updates.

For more information, go to

www.ICR.org

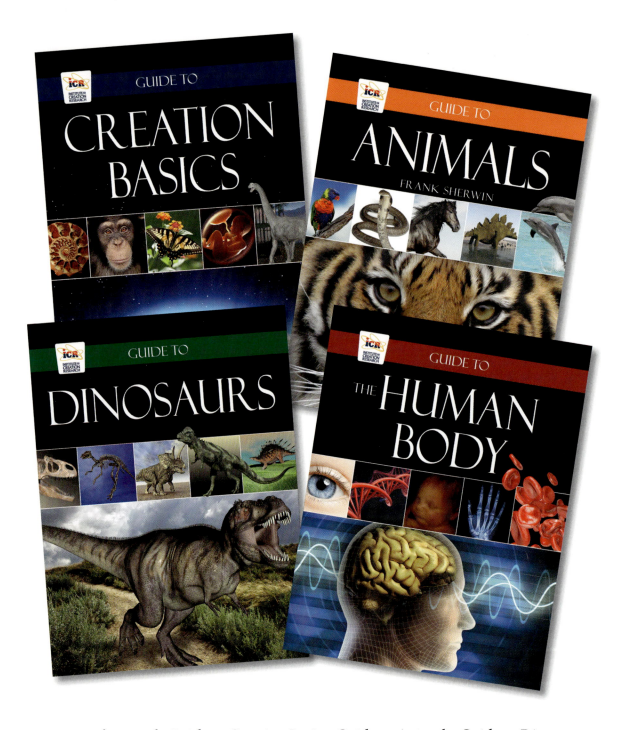

Get more facts with *Guide to Creation Basics, Guide to Animals, Guide to Dinosaurs,* and *Guide to the Human Body*! Designed for all ages, these hardcover books are loaded with cutting-edge scientific information and hundreds of full-color illustrations.

To order, call **800.628.7640** or visit **www.ICR.org/store**

Also available for Kindle, Nook, and through the iBookstore